children's
MINISTRY
in the 21st century

Group
Loveland, Colorado

www.group.com

Group resources actually work!

This Group resource incorporates our R.E.A.L. approach to ministry. It reinforces a growing friendship with Jesus, encourages long-term learning, and results in life transformation, because it's

Relational
Learner-to-learner interaction enhances learning and builds Christian friendships.

Experiential
What learners experience through discussion and action sticks with them up to 9 times longer than what they simply hear or read.

Applicable
The aim of Christian education is to equip learners to be both hearers and doers of God's Word.

Learner-based
Learners understand and retain more when the learning process takes into consideration how they learn best.

Credits
Contributing Authors: Ty Bryant, Rick Chromey, Heather Dunn, Debbie Gowensmith, Dale Hudson, Craig Jutila, Carmen Kamrath, Janna Kinner, Scott Kinner, Becki Manni, Steve Parolini, Sondra Saunders, Larry Shallenberger, Sharyn Spradlin, Pat Verbal, Jim Wideman, Dana Wilkerson, and Vicki L.O. Witte
Editors: Heather Dunn, Amber Van Schooneveld, and Ann Marie Rozum
Creative Development Editor: Christine Yount Jones
Chief Creative Officer: Joani Schultz
Copy Editor: Ann Jahns
Art Director: Josh Emrich
Print Production Artist: Julia Martin
Illustrator: Josh Emrich
Cover Art Directors/Designers: Josh Emrich and Veronica Lucas
Cover Illustrators: Josh Emrich and Veronica Lucas
Production Manager: DeAnne Lear

Library of Congress Cataloging-in-Publication Data
Children's ministry in the 21st century : the encyclopedia of practical ideas.
    p. cm.
 ISBN-13: 978-0-7644-3389-4 (pbk. : alk. paper)
1. Church work with children. I. Group Publishing.
 BV639.C4C435 2006
 259'.22--dc22

                    2006027868

15 14 13 12 11 10   21 20 19 18 17 16
Printed in the United States of America.

Contents

CONTRIBUTORS

Ty Bryant is the pastor for 4th through 6th grades at Perimeter Church in Duluth, Georgia. Because he became a follower of Jesus Christ during his preteen years, Ty is motivated to reach this age group with the gospel that has changed his life. He resides in Georgia with his cat, Stella.

Rick Chromey is professor of youth and family ministry at Kentucky Christian University in Grayson, Kentucky. In nearly a quarter of a century of professional youth ministry, Rick has served churches and colleges as a youth and children's pastor, professor, and trainer. Currently a doctoral candidate at George Fox Evangelical Seminary, Rick has authored two books, *Youth Ministry in Small Churches* and *Children's Ministry Guide for Smaller Churches*. He's also a regular contributor and columnist for Children's Ministry Magazine. He and his wife, Patty, have two children.

Heather Dunn is the children's product developer for Group Publishing. She started volunteering in children's ministry in her teens and has continued her involvement ever since. Her first career was in education. During the 20 years before coming to Group, she served as children's minister in three different churches. Heather is the creator of Group's exciting new JabberMat. She and her husband, Ken, have two adult children.

Dale Hudson has served in children's ministry for more than 17 years. His ministry to children has received recognition in numerous newspaper, magazine, and television reports, including TIME magazine, Christianity Today magazine, and ABC. He is the children's director at Central Christian Church in Las Vegas, Nevada. Dale and his wife, Pamela, have two sons.

Craig Jutila is the children's pastor at Saddleback Church in Lake Forest, California, where he leads a dynamic staff of 30 ministers and directors, more than 1,000 volunteers, and 4,500 children weekly. Craig is the founder of empoweringkids.net, a company designed to encourage, equip, energize, and empower other children's ministry leaders. Craig has written several articles, curricula, and books, the most notable from Group Publishing, including *Leadership Essentials for Children's Ministry, The Growing Leader: Healthy Essentials for Children's Ministry,* and *2-Minute Encouragers for Teachers.* Craig and his wife have three children.

Carmen Kamrath is the associate editor for Children's Ministry Magazine. She has a master's degree in education and has more than 15 years experience serving as a children's pastor in Arizona and Colorado. Carmen and her husband, Dan, have three children and live in Loveland, Colorado.

Sondra Saunders is the senior preschool/children's minister at Prestonwood Baptist Church in Dallas, Texas, and has served there for 27 years. She has been in the ministry for 44 years, and Prestonwood is one of four churches where she has served. Sondra has taught leadership conferences in numerous states and is a former Children's Ministry Magazine columnist.

Sharyn Spradlin has specialized in ministry for children, youth, and families for more than 20 years. She serves as a ministry coach for a Korean-American congregation (Hunjae Community Church of Seattle). She is a long-time contributor to Children's Ministry Magazine and a veteran presenter for Children's Ministry Magazine Live workshops.

Pat Verbal is the founder of Ministry to Today's Child. She is passionate about sharing her 20 years of pastoral experience with today's parents and teachers. Pat is a featured columnist for Children's Ministry Magazine and Teach Kids! magazine. She has co-authored 10 books, including *Special Needs, Special Ministry,* which is a bestseller among churches seeking to serve children with disabilities. Pat holds an MA from the Haggard School of Theology at Azusa Pacific University, where she served on the Council for Church Leaders.

Jim Wideman has served as a children's pastor for more than 28 years. He has created many resources for children's ministry, authored numerous books and magazine articles, and hosted *the club* children's ministry leadership audio series. Jim also has received the "Excellence in Children's Ministry" award and Children's Ministry Magazine's "Pioneers of the Decade" award. Currently, Jim serves at Church on the Move in Tulsa, Oklahoma, reaching more than 4,000 children weekly. Jim and Julie, his wife of 28 years, have two daughters, Yancy and Whitney.

FOREWORD

Welcome to *Children's Ministry in the 21st Century: The Encyclopedia of Practical Ideas.*

The fact that you picked up this book in the first place says a lot about you. You're committed to children, and you're committed to God. You obviously care about pursuing the most effective, trend-sensitive, need-meeting children's ministry possible—or you wouldn't be reading this book. You care about making the gospel relevant to kids and connecting with them in ways that are culturally relevant—ways they'll understand and hear so God can invade their lives.

Everything around us is changing. Culture. Kids. Families. Ministry methods. How can we keep up?

You've most likely heard the tongue-in-cheek use of the verse "We shall not all sleep for we shall be changed" in the nursery. It's highly likely that verse could be used throughout our entire children's ministries! Change. We're moving at what seems like the speed of light at times, and it affects our ministry today and tomorrow.

That's what this book is about. We asked top children's ministers to dive into the information you need, to flesh it out with their years of experience, and to guide us as we move into the 21st century. So, in the next pages of this book, you'll hear from experts such as Pat Verbal, Craig Jutila, Jim Wideman, Rick Chromey, and more. The people whose words and ideas appear in this book are wise students of kids, their culture, and making the gospel relevant for today.

We believe that God passionately loves children and has a special place in his heart for them. We believe that children are the church of today and deserve every attention and effort that's possible in order to share with them the love of God. We believe kids can have a thriving, wonderful relationship with Jesus and that they need Jesus' friends like you to help them.

That's why we've packed this book with 10 essays and dozens of practical ideas. You'll find tools, tips, activities, events, programs, creative ideas, and more after each essay that'll help you apply what you've just learned.

Our prayer is that as you use this book, you'll connect with kids in a way you never have before. Our hope is that the ideas and concepts in this book will teach you the secret kid-speak you need to impact this generation for Christ. May God bless you as you reach out to the most precious people on earth—kids!

Christine Yount Jones
Group's Children's Ministry Champion

USING THIS RESOURCE

We've compiled this book to be your encyclopedia for the new face of children's ministry in the 21st century.

We've highlighted eight specific trends in culture and ministry, such as technology, emerging family ministries, and the postmodern church, which are crucial for leaders of children to understand and apply. And we'll help you do both.

Each chapter has two parts. The first section of each chapter includes essays from experts in children's ministry to help you understand each new trend and how it affects your children and ministry. The second section, called "Try This," provides practical activities for applying what you've discovered—great answers to the question, "So what can I do about this in my ministry?"

The "Try This" sections will give you fresh ideas for events, games, small groups, worship, discussion starters, object lessons, the arts, outreach, and on and on. You'll see the "OK to copy" icon **OK** on pages where you'll distribute copies either to individual students or to groups.

Through this volume, you'll see your children's spiritual lives in a new light and understand who they really are with a fresh perspective. And you'll gain valuable, practical, and innovative ideas that will inspire your students to develop a life-transforming relationship with the Messiah and King.

Our prayer is that this tool will encourage you and strengthen your ministry as you serve God by loving children. May God work through you and your ministry in ways you can't yet even imagine!

CHAPTER

1

Not of This World

THE TIMES THEY ARE A-CHANGIN'

BY RICK CHROMEY

We live in a world of unbelievable change.

A decade now seems like a century.

Remember 1995? Back when the web was a spider's home. Back when mail was paper and phones had cords. Back when Spam came in a can.

In 1994 Netscape permitted broad Internet access and the whole world went "e." Snail mail morphed into e-mail. Cell phones replaced land lines and became microcomputers and televisions. Digital downloads, blogs, iPods, and satellite television reinvented communication and entertainment industries. Wi-Fi (wireless) created instant global connectivity.

We've become a culture of infinite connections via the Web. From MySpace to Amazon to Google to Wikipedia, we connect and commune through text-messaging, blogs, and chats. The technological ABCs abound. CD-R. DVD. GPS. AVI. MPEG. JPEG. MP3. In a cordless, wireless culture the frontier is cyberspace, and every human institution (politics, entertainment, education, commerce, church) is impacted.

In the words of best-selling author Thomas Friedman, the "world is flat." The rise of Web technology, wireless communications, and virtual reality has changed cultural rules, demolished hierarchical authority, and eliminated walls of class or creed. Have modem, will travel. The greatest indicator of poverty or ignorance or cultural relevance is Web connectivity (aka the "digital divide").

Either you're online or you're not.

Consequently, children's ministries that blossomed in the 1980s and 1990s are facing new paradigms. What worked five years ago now fails to attract or educate. Many churches (and their children's ministries) are disconnected, unplugged, or offline from their own neighborhoods, families, and cultural context.

CAN YOU HEAR ME NOW?
(THE RISE OF NEW CULTURAL LANGUAGES)

We reside in a *post*modern world.

For over five centuries, our culture operated within modern frames. Technological innovation—namely the printing press and the mechanized clock—shattered the chains of the Dark Ages. Modernity, via new structures and communication tools, emerged through the Renaissance and Reformation, Enlightenment and Industrial Revolution.

In a modern world, the church reflected this machine/word culture. The Bible was printed in chapter and verse. Denominations emerged (different strokes for different folks). Print and words reigned through sermon, hymn, and lesson. The church (like culture) mechanized its message via principles and purposes, sequence and science.

Modern children's ministries operated within calendar seasons, word formats, and passive learning models. Children memorized a book (the Bible). They learned in age-graded classrooms and within authoritative systems. From Sunday school to children's church, kids were taught "belief in a box." Church was a place, an answer, or a destination. Faith was a frame.

But that world is fading—fast!

Three technological advances in the 20th century have introduced a global, postmodern, post-Christian cultural shift: television, cellular phones, and the Internet. Television launched a culture of image, experience, and virtual reality. Cell and Web technology shaped new communication formats with instant, global, and relational consequence.

As a result, children's ministries of the 21st century will reinvent themselves around relationships, images, and experiences that are 24/7/365, where faith is a personal, dynamic journey. The Word will be image. Flesh and blood. Experiential. In a high-tech culture, people value a high-touch connection.

Can you hear me now? Technology releases new cultural tones and dialects. We're talking but kids don't understand. A cultural language—or how we interact or operate within social frameworks—is intricately tied to technology.

Modern (1500–1990)	VS.	Postmodern (1990–)
Printing Press, Mechanized Clock		**Television, Cell Phone, Internet**
"I think, therefore I am." -Rene Descartes		*"Can we all get along?"* -Rodney King
"Here I stand." -Martin Luther		*"I still haven't found what I'm looking for."* -Bono, U2

Mechanized	System	**Relational**	Community
	Science		Connection
	Class/Creed		Tolerance
	Industry		Global
	Logic		

Passive	Lecture/ Sermon	**Experiential**	Authentic
	Hierarchical		Participatory
	"In the Box"		Extreme
	Destination		Journey
	Religious		Spiritual

Word	Literacy	**Experiential**	Digital
	Print		Instant/Live
	Audio		Visual Multi-task
	Mono-task		Fluid
	Foundational		Imaginative

In Acts 2, on the day of Pentecost, the church was born. Ironically, its greatest issue was communication. These largely illiterate Jews faced a multilingual audience. According to Scripture, the apostles were gifted by the Holy Spirit to speak the people's language (including unique dialects). This miracle was not of man, but of the Holy Spirit.

Similarly, children's ministries must recognize that human purpose, program, or power will fail. Only the Holy Spirit enables us to speak culturally relevant messages and to live our faith in a dark, carnal world.

Fortunately our culture is hungry for God.

And children are the most receptive to spirituality.

S-P-I-R-I-T

Astronauts are "sailors" (*naut*) of the "stars" (*astro*). However, God calls his leaders to different worlds. Leonard Sweet suggests that postmodern Christians are "pneumanauts," or "sailors" (*naut*) of the "Spirit" (*pneuma*). We're in the world, yet not of it. We fearlessly soar above it.

The emerging postmodern culture spells "S-P-I-R-I-T," and children's ministries in the 21st century must learn to sail this new frontier.

Sensory

Postmodern culture welcomes experiences and defines truth through life. Moderns tapped eyes and ears, but postmoderns have rediscovered smell, taste, and touch. The modern church reduced Jesus to a book, creed, or idea. The postmodern church will literally "re-incarnate" Jesus as "flesh."

Need a metaphor? Most children's ministries resemble a McDonald's drive-through. Kids line up, order, and exit. It's a fast-food faith. But what if we operated more like a Rainforest Cafe? Life's jungle creates a sensory sanctuary. Can you help kids taste God? smell Jesus? touch the Spirit?

Pluralistic

Postmodern culture is tolerant. It's a "whatever" world. Truth is relative to personal experience. Where moderns lived in a black and white or gray culture, postmoderns question the colors altogether. They see "blight" or "whack" instead. To a modern, the Outback Steakhouse motto, "No rules. Just right." is an oxymoron. To a postmodern, it makes perfect sense.

Children's ministries will face increasing pressure to communicate Jesus as "*the* way, *the* truth, and *the* life" (John 14:6, emphasis added) to a post-Christian culture. Consequently, we must honor faith's journey, including its doubts, discouragements, and dryness. Celebrate milestones. Create conversations. Carve memories. Console hardships.

Faith is an *Amazing Race* where, like passengers on Southwest Airlines, believers are "now free to move about" the kingdom. Tolerance doesn't mean endorsement but divine empathy.

Image-Driven

Our culture thinks with its eyes.

Nike? A *swoosh* symbol. McDonald's? Golden arches. Television single-handedly morphed a word world into an image culture. iPods aren't a nifty fad. They're the wave of the future: personalized, portable television.

In John 1:1, the Greek word for *Word* is *logos*. Moderns love the word. Postmoderns long for "logo." They like to brand (tattoos). They don't seek a "red letter" Bible but desire metaphor, story, and "eye-deas."

Here's a question: How does your children's ministry brand itself? What mark do you leave on kids? What do your children "see" at church—on the walls, the PowerPoint, the handouts? Is your image tarnished? worn? irrelevant?

Reality

Reality television is no fad.

To a modern, reality is scientific and logical. Pictures don't lie. Truth is graspable. Life's problems have answers. But postmoderns feel otherwise. Technology creates alternative, virtual realities. What's "real"? What's "true"? Who knows? Consequently, postmodern culture thrives on authentic "get real" moments. It's "life unscripted" (Fox Reality channel) or the "real thing" (Coca-Cola).

Either you're "real" to your children, or you're a spiritual hologram. Do they know your insecurities, pain, or troubles (and vice versa)? *Fear Factor* is a top show among elementary boys. What's the "fear factor" of your children's ministry? In a video game culture, kids want to be "in the game."

So keep it real.

International

We live in global community.

A tsunami sparks worldwide philanthropy. A terror plot has international implications. The world is getting smaller. The modern operated within local contexts. Until television, news traveled by ear or print. Today we make instantaneous global connections. Tech support is a call to Singapore. Even my small Kentucky town boasts Chinese, Mexican, and Italian restaurants.

In global culture, tomorrow's children's ministries must refocus on the Great Go-Mission (Matthew 28:18-20). Every child is a missionary. Imagine the opportunity a mouse and modem afford. Download Google Earth and see the world.

Tech-Reliant

Today's children have grown within a tech-friendly climate. They're natives to a high-tech birthright (most born since 1960). Postmoderns find comfort in technology, not fear. They discover perfect pitch with cords.

Megatrends author John Naisbitt predicted that a high-tech culture creates high-touch opportunity. The two most accessed Internet categories are porn and dating. In a plastic world, intimacy is a driving need. Technology creates relational hunger.

Unfortunately, few children's ministries help families navigate technological landmines. Are we preparing for tomorrow's tech advances? Human engineering, bioterror, and identity theft will continue to flourish. Most transactions (loans, food, entertainment) will happen in cyberspace. Tomorrow's universities will be online, as modern seat-based, time-based institutions become increasingly irrelevant.

THE CULTURAL SWAMP: "IN IT? OF IT? WITH IT?"

In a postmodern world, cultural change is fluid. The trends that once took years to come and go rise and fall in weeks and days. Culture tends toward the extreme. Sexuality, violence, and profanity mark the television landscape. The Internet is flooded with pornography, gambling, and danger.

In this polluted cultural swamp, children grow.

Also troublesome is that for the first time since A.D. 325—when

Constantine charted a Christian empire—we're now living in a post-Christian world. Christianity's influence—politically, educationally, philosophically—is largely questioned, ridiculed, or dismissed.

Historically, the church responds to cultural sewage through *isolation*, choosing separation or a subculture that parallels secular society. *Christian* education. *Christian* entertainment. *Christian* business. Separation from the world insulates and provides understandable security.

Conversely, some Christian families adopt cultural *immersion*. Such Christian homes allow questionable television shows, music, and books (not to mention behavior). These homes present problems for children's ministries who attract children deeply stained by cultural pollutants. When Bobby launches the "F" word at home, his parents smirk, but at church his flowery language offends.

It's a "kagoy" world. A culture where "kids are getting older younger." Many parents culturally baptize their children through questionable fashion, entertainment, or behavioral choices (alcohol, violence, or even sexual activity). Other well-meaning parents immerse preteen kids in activities—beauty pageants, talent contests, or sports—that pressure, push, and pull them into adult venues, values, and even vices.

Consequently, neither isolation nor immersion is ultimately healthy.

So what's the solution to this cultural swamp?

A positive approach is to *inoculate* children against offensive content. An inoculation actually injects the virus into the system to build immunity. Similarly, children's ministries (and parents) can immunize kids against cultural toxins.

Postmodern culture encourages experiential truth and embraces relativism. In a whatever, wherever world, children will need a Christ-centered compass that always points them home. Nevertheless, small doses of alternative truth, questionable behavior, and even inappropriate language—within proper age and family contexts—can ultimately build immunity (discernment and right decisions) against later adoption of these same cultural pollutants.

For example, children *will* hear offensive language. The isolationist would cover Junior's ears. The immersionist would look away. Those choosing inoculation would frame the language within context to develop teachable moments. A preschooler flaunting his "middle finger" is different than a fifth-grader doing the same. The question isn't what happened, but why.

Children's ministries can only inoculate to a point. Most immunization is family-based. We cannot alter family values unless granted permission.

Inoculation is healthy, but there is a higher path.

Jesus called his disciples—through his own example—to live *incarnationally* within culture. *Incarnational* means sensing pain and stepping into tragedy to enact change. It's being light or salt. It's John 3:16. Every evil is an expression of emptiness and envy (James 4:1-3). Profanity, violence, sensuality, abuse, and addiction are simply bandages. Inoculation builds immunity, but incarnational living leads to victory. Immunity prevents cultural stains, but incarnational living loves the stained.

Grace is the word.

Children, especially those who are culturally stained, are open to incarnational strategies that evoke grace, relationship, worth, and security. A children's ministry that empathizes with hurt children, builds bridges, loves unconditionally, and lifts kids to better life decisions (in speech, purity, behavior, values) is one that ultimately rescues and redeems.

Incarnational children's ministry will be criticized, especially from isolationists. "We don't want bad language at church!" "That's devil's music!" "*That* movie isn't a good one." But grace isn't nice, fair, or even rational (something isolationist critics fail to recognize).

Does that mean anything goes?

Absolutely not.

A positive children's ministry that leads incarnationally won't license profanity or inappropriate activity. However, it will empathize and encourage better behavior (and enact logical consequences for *continuous* misbehavior). A child who repeatedly hits others cannot be tolerated or trusted within a classroom. Likewise kids who constantly use profanity or suggestive gestures—despite admonishment—must face the consequence (including suspension from activities).

Incarnational children's ministry partners with families to teach improved parenting skill and strategy. It *feels* with a family to understand why children act up or out. It inoculates families against wider cultural toxins through biblical teaching. Ultimately, it lives *grace*. Wild forgiveness. Outrageous love. Unlimited favor.

SEEING CULTURE WITH 3-D VISION

Because postmodern society speaks new languages of the "spirit," many cultural manifestations (arising from a base humanity) reflect the vile, violent, and vain. Teach your children to use 3-D glasses in regard to culture.

Dialogue

For years, we've slowly inoculated our children against cultural influences through conversation. Recently, an innocent late-night TV show went to a *Girls Gone Wild* commercial. We scrambled to change the channel, but our kids saw several images of girls in sexual poses. For several minutes, we dialogued on the degradation of pornography. My son got the point. "Mom," he said, "I don't want to look at anything that makes a girl less than a woman."

Children's ministries must regularly, and appropriately, discuss cultural influences and expressions. Kids are watching. Many already know too much. Family television hours are littered with language most adults learned on playgrounds. Cable television and home videos introduced unedited content to families. Therefore, family conversation is crucial (because most "offensive" influences happen at home or school).

Discernment

The reason many children are culturally crippled is that they lack discernment. Adult caregivers either respond to cultural sewage with isolation or immersion. Isolationists may keep their kids "innocent" but also ignorant. Immersionists may raise "sophisticated" children, but in reality they're stained. Neither extreme teaches discernment, and both ultimately fail.

Remember the song "Oh Be Careful, Little Eyes, What You See"? The key word is *careful*. That's discernment. Discernment recognizes the difference between right and wrong, good and bad, pure and impure. My son's reaction to media sexuality? He chooses to bury his head. We don't have to tell him, he just does it. He's learning discernment.

Children's ministries have a tremendous responsibility to teach discernment. It's not enough to merely say "don't look." We must help children understand why "not looking" is the best choice. In a postmodern culture, anything goes. But, as Paul penned to the

Corinthians (who lived in a corrupt, openly pornographic society): "'I am allowed to do anything'—but not everything is beneficial" (1 Corinthians 10:23).

What's beneficial is always best.

Discipline

Ultimately, dialogue and discernment are meaningless without commitment to discipline. A disciplined life—a mark of maturity—recognizes evil and has strategies for escape. Neither isolationist nor immersionist approaches are rooted in discipline. To sever and separate from culture is difficult but not impossible (consider the Amish). Immersionists eschew discipline altogether.

Conversely, the disciplined life is foundational to inoculationists, but freeing to incarnationalists. Those immune to cultural toxins will recognize filth and walk clear. The incarnationalist, however, will lead the addicted or abused victims of cultural sewage to cleansing in Christ. He travels with immunity, but also victory.

Many families lack the discipline to grow incarnational, spiritually mature children on their own. Consequently, children's ministries must resource, equip, and inspire parents hungry for support. The truth is that a children's ministry can teach cultural discernment. However, the family context is where a disciplined life truly grows. A child raised in an undisciplined (immersionist or isolationist) home may learn some discernment at church but ultimately bows to the family life.

"Kagoy"

In a culture where kids grow older at younger ages, it's easy for children's ministers to be discouraged. But "kagoy" is also strength. Kids don't make choices from a vacuum. If influential adults—primarily in the plastic realm of media—can sway fashion and entertainment choice, imagine what flesh and blood can do.

I've got a secret for you.

You matter.

And you're "Jesus" to this generation.

Aren't you relieved Jesus didn't isolate himself in heaven? Aren't you thankful he didn't wantonly wallow in sin, either? Neither choice would provide salvation. Rather, Jesus found cultural immunity through his knowledge of Scripture, his community of faith, and his love for God. Consequently, Jesus could touch lepers, dine with prostitutes, turn water into wine, and, in righteous rage, turn the temple's tables.

Jesus built relationships, created powerful and positive experiences, and was the "image" of God (Colossians 1:15).

He spoke the cultural language of the time. He still speaks ours today.

Jesus lived in the world, though not of it. He was both within and above it.

And you can be, too.

So listen to the children. Who influences them? What movies excite? What music inspires? Then use these cultural icons as teaching bridges. When kids speak profanity or hit others, realize that hurt people hurt people. Where there is sin, a savior is needed.

And that's why Jesus came.

And that's why he's sending you.

Really, you *do* matter.

Tip

In every issue of Children's Ministry Magazine, you'll find a "Keeping Current" section. This resource will keep you up to date with trends, research, and media that affect your children.

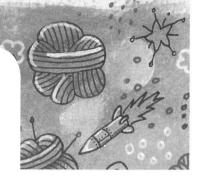

Try This

BY LARRY SHALLENBERGER

PLAYLIST

Here's an idea for an ongoing lesson you can use to help preteens evaluate whether the music they listen to supports their Christian values. Build this activity into your lesson, or use this activity if you have extra time.

Say: **Music is a big part of our lives, even here at church! We worship God with music, and sometimes we listen to music to feel energized or maybe to relax. But how do we know whether the music we choose is pleasing to God? Let's find out by putting some of our favorite songs to the test.**

Have children list their favorite songs. These can be songs they hear on the radio, songs they sing in a choir, or even campfire songs. Explain that each time you meet for the next several months, you'll all listen to one of the songs (or, if you'd rather dedicate only one lesson to this activity, explain that you'll listen to all the songs during your next meeting). When they've finished, have kids give their lists of songs to you. During the following week, choose one of the songs listed and obtain a recording of the song by either borrowing a CD or legally downloading the song from a Web-based store such as www.itunes .com, www.napster.com, or www.songtouch.com. And while you're on the Internet, perform a Web search to find and print that song's lyrics.

Next, photocopy the "Worthy Words?" handout on page 23 so that each child will have one.

During the next class, pass out lyrics sheets or show the lyrics on an overhead so kids can follow along, and play the song on the CD. Then hand out the "Worthy Words?" handout, and have kids complete it with a partner. Afterward, have all kids participate in the following discussion:

For Extra Impact

Check with the local skating rink to see if kids are allowed to pick songs the DJ plays. If so, reserve the rink for your class for a few hours one evening, and let kids decide on the music!

- **Will this song help or hurt your friendship with Jesus? Is it just a "fun" song that really doesn't make a difference? Explain.**
- **If Jesus visited your house, would you feel comfortable playing this song while he was there? Why or why not?**

WORTHY WORDS?

NAME OF SONG: _____

"And now, dear brothers and sisters, one final thing. Fix your thoughts on what is true, and honorable, and right, and pure, and lovely, and admirable. Think about things that are excellent and worthy of praise" (Philippians 4:8).

Draw a picture that shows what this song is about.

Does this song help you think about things that are important to God? Why or why not?

_____
_____
_____
_____

Does this song say anything about relationships? If so, does it match up with how God says we should treat each other?

_____
_____
_____
_____

Do you like the song? Circle the face that shows your thoughts about the words and the style of music.

Activity 2

FAMILY MOVIE NIGHT

Plan an evening out with the kids in your class—and their families! When a new kids' movie comes to the theater, buy a block of tickets that families can purchase from you. Arrange to meet at someone's home (or even a restaurant!) after the movie for dessert and a group discussion.

Kids will remember the fun time you had together as a family for years to come. This is also a great way for parents to make friends with other parents of children the same age as their kids.

Use the following questions to prompt lively dialogue. Be sure kids have a chance to share their opinions!

- **What did you like best about the movie?**
- **Do you think Jesus would object to any part of the movie? Why or why not?**
- **Which character in the story did you like the most? the least? Why?**
- **If you were the director of this movie, what would you change?**
- **Would you recommend this movie to other families you know? Why or why not?**
- **Why is it important that we think about what movies we watch?**

For more ideas about church movie nights, check out Group's *More Than a Movie*. You'll find ideas for organizing get-togethers that combine movies, faith conversations, and hands-on activities.

Activity 3

SHARING WISDOM

Try this intergenerational activity that gets kids and adults to discuss faith together. Arrange to have your children's Sunday school class visit an adult Sunday school class to learn about their faith.

Help younger children prepare questions ahead of time concerning what God is like. For instance, they might ask: "Does God have a birthday?" or "How is God everywhere?" List their questions on a piece of paper.

Older students might prepare questions that are more doctrinal in nature, such as "Can you help me understand the Trinity?" or ethical questions, such as "How did you deal with temptation at our age?" Have these students write their questions on index cards to bring to the meeting.

Before adults and kids meet, arrange chairs in a circle so everyone can see each other and there isn't an "audience vs. panel" feel. During the sharing time, serve yummy snacks to break the ice and facilitate introduction between the children and the adults. Then give kids a chance to benefit from the wisdom and experience of the adults. You might need to read questions aloud for the younger kids, but allow older children to ask the adults their questions.

For added impact, use a video recorder to capture the discussions. That way, you can use parts of the dialogue during later lessons.

Here are tips to help children of different ages get involved:

- Let younger children help prepare and serve snacks to the adults.
- Older children can operate the video camera if you use one.
- If you're worried about younger children getting shy or quiet in front of adults, consider prerecording their questions before the interview. Then play the recording during the sharing time, pausing after each question so an adult can answer.

Activity 4

CURRENT EVENT SCAVENGER HUNT

This simple activity will help your children look at current events through God's point of view.

Before class, collect a large pile of the past week's newspapers or newsmagazines. Tape several pieces of newsprint to the wall. Use a marker to label each sheet of newsprint with a different header:

Things that make God happy

Things that demonstrate God's love

Things that don't show God's love

Things that draw people away from God

Have kids look through the newspapers and magazines to find stories that fit in one of the four categories. Have them clip the articles and use glue sticks to fasten them to the appropriate newsprint.

After kids have had several minutes to catalog their stories, collect the scissors and glue. Ask:

- **Which type of article was the easiest to find? Which was the hardest to find?**
- **Which news story do you think makes God the happiest? Why?**
- **Which news story do you think makes God the saddest? Why?**

Have someone read aloud 1 Timothy 2:1-4. Ask:

- **Why is it important to pray over the things happening in our world today?**
- **Why do you think God asks us specifically to pray for our leaders?**

Lead the children in a time of prayer. Remind them to thank God for the things that make him happy and to pray that God would remind our leadership to make choices that help people.

Tips to enhance this activity:

- When teaching younger children, use magazines with lots of colorful pictures rather than a newsmagazine. Help kids cut out pictures of people who are making God happy and pictures of people who are making God sad. Have the children make collages of these two themes using poster board.
- Make this an ongoing project with your older classrooms. Each week give the kids a theme for their current event, such as "stories about people who are serving others." Tell the children to either clip a news story or to print out a Web page from a news Web site. Begin each class by allowing the kids to share their news story with a partner, and add a brief prayer to ask God to have his hand in the news of the week.

Activity 5

CHOICES GAME

Use this board game to help children understand that their choices have consequences.

To make the game board large enough for children to stand on, copy the "Choices Game" onto an overhead transparency. Tape a large piece of butcher paper (or even several pieces taped together) to a wall. Use an overhead projector to magnify the transparency image onto the butcher paper. Trace the image with a wide marker. Remove the butcher paper from the wall and set it on the floor of your classroom, image-side up.

Next, create two "Consequence" Decks:

Positive Consequence: Using 10 index cards (one for each sentence), write 10 sentences such as "Way to go! Move ahead two steps" or "Great job! Jump to the next space." Vary the affirmations and the amount for spaces rewarded.

Negative Consequence: Using 10 more index cards, write 10 sentences such as "Uh-oh, that wasn't your best option. Go back one space" or "Oops! That wasn't such a good idea. Lose one turn."

Finally, make a "Situation" Deck. Using a third stack of index cards, write several choices your children might face. These should be formed as "Will I…" questions. For example, you might write, "Will I obey my mom when she tells me to clean my room?" or "Will I cheat on a math test?"

Place a piece of tape on the front and back of a coin. Write "yes" on one side and "no" on the other. Now you're ready to play!

Have each child remove his or her shoes and stand on one of the game spaces.

To start the game, the youngest child draws a Situation Card and reads it aloud. Then he or she flips the coin—whether it lands with the "yes" or "no" face up, he or she will draw from the deck that corresponds to that choice and move accordingly. Play continues to the right. As each situation card is read, ask the class one or two of the following questions:

- **Would it be easy or hard to make the right choice in this situation? Why?**
- **Have you ever faced this choice in real life? What did you do?**
- **Who could you turn to for help in making the right decision?**

After playing a round or two, gather the kids and have a volunteer read aloud Ephesians 6:11. Ask:

- **How did you feel when you didn't get to make your own choice? How is that like following someone's example instead of making your own decisions?**
- **How did you feel when you got to move forward on the board? How about when you had to move backward?**
- **How do our everyday choices move us "forward" or "backward"?**
- **How can "putting on God's armor" help us move in the right direction?**

Here are more options for you to use to enhance this activity:

- Older children can help create and trace their own giant game board, and they can invent their own situation cards.
- Designate one space as the "end" space on the game board, and have children play until they reach this space. (Have several children start on the same space.)
- If space is an issue, just copy the game board onto poster board and use random items as game pieces.

Activity 6

ADOPT A MISSIONARY PEN PAL

In his lead-in to this chapter, Rick Chromey explained that today's children have a more international perspective than their counterparts of earlier generations. Use this service project as a way to meet the needs of missionary children as you help your kids learn about other cultures.

Contact your church's missionary board and obtain names and e-mail addresses of missionary children whose families your church supports. In class, pass out the names and addresses and help your students write letters to those children. Encourage your kids to make a connection with the missionary children by describing their own hobbies and their favorite foods and asking the missionary children what their favorite foods and hobbies are. If you have younger children in your class, be prepared to help write the children's questions and comments.

If you have a computer in class, send the e-mails together from a church e-mail account. If not, ask parents to help their children send the e-mails from home.

Each time you receive a response from a missionary child, read the letter aloud to the class and post it on a bulletin board with an arrow pointing to the country it came from (and the child's photo, if you have it). Encourage your kids to maintain a relationship with their new missionary friends by writing back each time they receive an e-mail.

Use these suggestions to take this activity to the next level:

- Encourage the kids in your class to save money to purchase small gifts for the missionary children—like comic books or school supplies.
- Bring encyclopedias or Web articles to class to help your kids learn more about the country and culture that the missionary children live in.
- Overcome the limited literacy skills of younger ones by helping them record an audiotape message that you can mail to the missionary children.

Activity 7

PETER AND CORNELIUS

Use this devotional to help children understand that God wants us to share his love with all people.

Before class, collect small, inexpensive food items to represent a variety of ethnic food. For example, a bag of chow mein noodles can represent Chinese food; a can of tomato sauce can represent Italian food. Take care to gather a food item from several cultures and include unusual items or spices.

Wrap the food in a blanket, and place the blanket in the center of a table.

Read aloud Acts 10:9-16 from a children's Bible.

Say: **In Peter's culture, it was wrong for people who loved God to eat certain kinds of animals. People from Israel who were serious about being friends with God wouldn't even share meals with people who ate these animals. They called the animals unclean, even though it was God who created the animals! Because of this rule, Jewish people like Peter never made good friendships with people from other cultures.**

Open the blanket so kids can see the food. Hold up each food item, and let children guess which country the food came from.

Say: **God wanted Peter to build friendships with people from every culture. That's why God showed him a "menu" of food that people ate from all over the world. God gave his people permission to eat everything on the menu so they could make friends with others around the world. God wanted Peter to make friendships with people from every country so he could tell them about Jesus.** Ask:

- **How would you feel if God spoke to you in a dream to give you instructions?**
- **What keeps you from building friendships with people who are different from you?**
- **Why does God want us to build friendships with people who are different from us?**

Say: **God loves all people, no matter what country they live in or what culture they belong to. He wants us to build friendships with everyone so we can tell everyone about him.**

"Bam!" Kick up this lesson by serving the children a meal from another culture. Bring in Chinese takeout, tacos, or even small portions of spaghetti.

Activity 8

STANDING UP FOR GOD AT SCHOOL

Use this lesson to help kids understand the importance of standing up for God's truth in school.

Before class, purchase yummy treats such as cupcakes and a small bag of healthy snacks such as carrots.

Open your Bible to Daniel 1, and explain to the children that Daniel and his people lived in a faraway country called Babylon. The king of this country didn't love God, and he and his people didn't follow God's rules.

Read aloud Daniel 1:1-8. Say: **Let's pretend you're all students in King Nebuchadnezzar's special school. The king wants you to work hard at school so someday you can lead his people. And the king wants you to eat the best food that he has.**

Pass out cupcakes to the whole class, but don't let them eat yet.

Say: **But those were the days when God had laws about which foods to eat. Daniel and his friends knew that God didn't want them to eat the king's food. The king ate certain foods that were against God's laws. So Daniel and his friends chose to stand up for God, and they obeyed him. They asked to be allowed to eat vegetables and water instead of the king's special food and drink.**

Take the cupcakes away from two or three children, and replace them with a handful of carrots. Invite the children to enjoy their snacks. After a moment, ask those with carrots:

- **How did it feel to watch the other children eat cupcakes while you ate vegetables?**

Ask everyone:

- **What are some ways that standing up for God makes you different from other kids?**
- **Is it easy or hard to stand up for God at school? Why?**
- **How can you stand up for God in school this week?**

Return the cupcakes to the kids who were given carrots. Say:
Daniel and his friends stood up for God and followed his rules, even when no one else did. I'm sure it wasn't easy; the king's food looked so good. But they wanted to stand up for God by obeying his good rules. And God blessed them.

Activity 9

THE FOUR I'S OF PARENTING

Isolate, immerse, inoculate, incarnate.

This short object lesson for parents will launch a spirited discussion on Christian parenting in your next adult Sunday school class or small group. Before your meeting, collect a box, a sponge, a bowl of water, a few candies that look like medicine tablets, and a baby doll.

Say: **Christian parents are concerned about the effects that culture can have on our children. We don't want our kids to pick up negative values and ideas that harm their relationship with God. One children's ministry expert suggests that whether we realize it or not, we adopt one of four responses in our parenting style.**

Pass around the box. Say: **Some of us build high walls of protection around our children. We don't want them exposed to anything that might harm them, so we keep them in a box,** *isolating* **them from all potentially negative influences.**

Next pass the sponge. Say: **Some parents go to the other extreme. They don't see what the big deal is, and they allow their children to soak up any experience they wish.** Drop the sponge in the bowl of water.

Now pass around the candy tablets. Say: **And a third group of parents attempt to inoculate their children from the negative effects of culture. They let their children experience culture to a certain point, coaching them along the way. But they aren't afraid to immunize with a firm "no" when they think their kids are getting too close to someone or something potentially harmful.**

Pass the baby. Say: **Finally, a fourth group of parents turn to an incarnational model of relating to culture. They train their children to see past the damaging parts of culture and to love the people in it with grace.**

Display all of the props in the center of the room. Ask:
- **Which of the four styles best describes your parenting style? Why?**
- **What are advantages and disadvantages of each style?**
- **Are different styles more appropriate for children of different ages? Why or why not?**
- **Which style do you think Jesus would adopt?**

Read aloud James 1:27. Ask:
- **How does this verse help explain the tension found in the incarnational model?**
- **Which of the four models best prepares our children for a lifetime of loving God and loving others? Explain.**

Activity 10

THE LOGO PSALMS

Today's kids respond to images and logos like no other generation. Try this simple art activity to get children thinking about what God is like. Before class, cut out a picture of the McDonald's golden arches and a Nike *swoosh*.

Say: **When we shop for things, we often look for pictures to help us find what we want to buy.** Hold up the picture of the golden arches. Ask:

• **What would we find near these arches?**

Hold up the picture of the Nike *swoosh*. Ask:

• **What would you find inside a store with this symbol in the window?**

Say: **These pictures tell us what the stores have to offer. The images are called logos, and we know what to expect when we see them. Let's make pictures, or logos, that could help people know what to expect about God.**

Set out art supplies and paper. Tell kids that they'll hear descriptions that psalmists of the Bible wrote about God, and they'll choose one of those descriptions to create a picture—or logo—showing what God is like. For example, Psalm 8:1 might prompt someone to draw a logo of a crown or the sun shining above the clouds. Have volunteer children each read aloud a picturesque psalm such as 8:1; 18:1-2; 23:1-4; or 47:1-2.

When kids have finished drawing, have them share their picture with a partner and discuss the following in pairs:

• **What do you hope others will learn about God when they see your logo?**

• **Why is it important to know what God is like?**

• **If God drew a logo representing you, what would it look like?**

Here's a hot idea: Use a scanner to transfer the kids' logos to iron-on decals, then iron the images onto T-shirts for them.

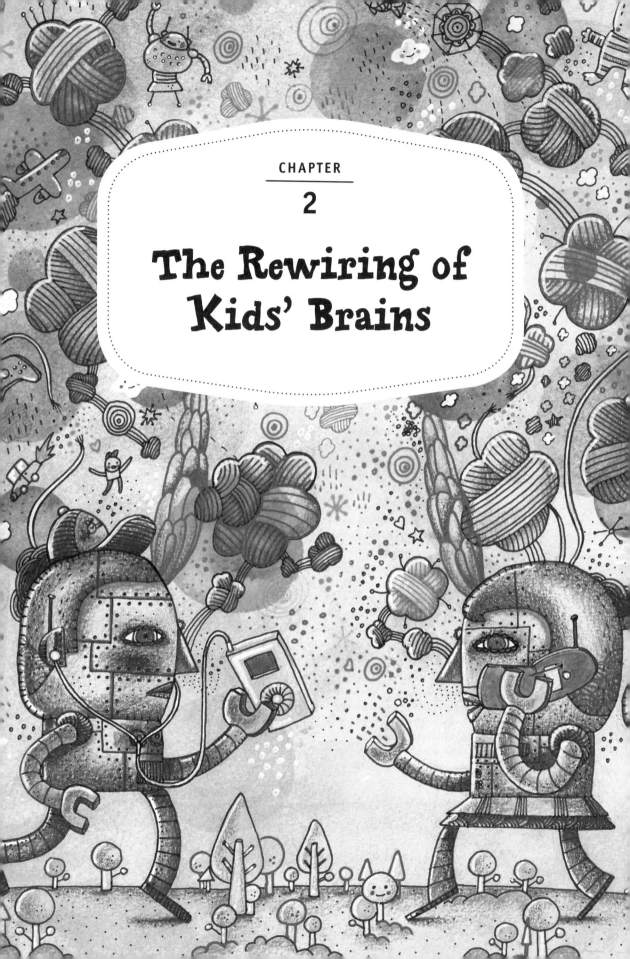

CHAPTER

2

The Rewiring of Kids' Brains

THE WIRED CHILD

BY DALE HUDSON

Remember your first cell phone? It was probably a far cry from today's slick, trendy phones that look more like fashion accessories than communication devices, but if you were like me, you congratulated yourself for owning cutting-edge technology.

When my son turned 13, he wanted a piece of the cutting edge, too—he convinced me that he had to have his own cell. And so, when Christmas rolled around, my wife and I bought him one. It was slick. It was slim. It was just what he wanted. But I hoped to have a little fun with him first, so I wrapped a clunky "dinosaur" of a cell phone (much like the first one I owned!) and placed it under the tree. I eagerly awaited his reaction to the joke Christmas morning—surely he would appreciate my clever wit!—but it was only when we used *that* phone to dial his *real* gift under the tree that his face changed from devastation to elation.

Why would a cutting-edge cell phone be so important to my son? It's because he belongs to Generation M. Generation M is one of several identifiers used to describe the media- and Internet-savvy consumer generation we're trying to reach for Christ. Market Wire reports that today's kids and teens are the first totally "wired" generation, and they're changing the world of marketing, technology, and communications as we knew it. Today's kids aren't just surrounded by media and technology—they live and breathe it every day.

Take a look into Generation M's world:
- 99 percent have a TV in their home.
- 97 percent have a VCR/DVD player.
- 86 percent have a personal computer in their home.
- 74 percent have Internet access.
- 31 percent have high-speed Internet access.
- 37 percent have their own TV in their room with cable or satellite.
- Millions of children have their own personal Web sites.

Generation M is immersed in technology—they live and breathe it. In fact, an independent study from the Kaiser Family Foundation explored the daily media usage of over 2,000 children ages 8 to 18. The results show that children are engaged with media for an average of 6.5 hours a day. Because they multi-task, many are cramming 8.5 hours of media usage into those 6.5 hours.

They aren't replacing "old" media; they're simply adding more media usage to their daily lives. Kevin Marks, software engineer and founding member of the Social Software Alliance, said it best: "My generation draws the Internet as a cloud that connects everyone; the younger generation experiences it as oxygen that supports their digital lives."

Technology is moving at the speed of light and carrying children along with it. World knowledge now doubles every 18 months. Moore's Law states that microprocessing speed doubles every 18 months. In fact, most of the stats I'm listing will soon be outdated. Technology is not a placid pond but a roaring rapids.

Cell phones made especially for kids are now hitting the market, and parents are purchasing them for children at younger and younger ages. Cars are made with built-in DVD players and screens in the back of each seat. Children's programming is available 24/7 on multiple television channels.

Welcome to the land of Generation M! We're called to connect them to Christ. How can we effectively fulfill this calling? Let's see what the Bible says: In 1 Chronicles 12:32, we are told about the men of Issachar, who "understood the signs of the times and knew the best course for Israel to take."

If we're going to be effective, we must be diligent to know the times in which we live and the culture of the children and families we're reaching out to. Let's take a look at how technology is rewiring kids' brains and how we can effectively minister to them.

THE REWIRING OF KIDS' BEHAVIOR

Kids are now wired to match the speed of the technology that drives their world:

- ***Kids seem uneasy when not stimulated by technology and media.*** For many kids, the cell phone must always be close by or they feel lost. The television has to be on at all times. The iPod must pump music into their ears no matter where they are. E-mail must be checked often lest an important message is missed.

   How can we effectively minister to these kids? Use the technology of their generation to reach out to them. Make them feel comfortable by using tools of their own media world to communicate with them.

- ***Many children imitate what they see in media and technology.*** Parents often see their children imitate some type of behavior from TV. Sometimes it's positive behavior like sharing or helping. But sometimes it's negative behavior like hitting or kicking.

   How can we effectively minister to them? Teach children to use media and technology but not be ruled by it. Teach children and parents to make wise choices about technology and media they'll expose themselves to. Teach them to look at media and technology with a Christian worldview.

- ***Kids' play is rewired.*** Children are wired to play! But today's kids turn more and more to technology—instead of tree houses, bicycles, or jump ropes—for play. Technology and media are the playground of choice for Generation M.

   Video game systems like PlayStation, Xbox 360, GameCube, and more are where many of them spend their time "playing." Media Wise reports that 87 percent of 8- to 17-year-old children play video games at home. The U.S. video game market reached nearly $10.5 billion in sales in 2005. Approximately 203 million video game units were sold in 2004 in the U.S.—up from 186 million video game units sold in 2003.

   How can we effectively minister to them? Enter their "playground"! Create a children's ministry Web site where children can be a part of online contests, play games, and vote for what's going to happen at upcoming services. Provide video games for them to play or areas where they can safely surf the

Web before your services begin. Use on-screen interactive games as a part of your services.

Come play with them, and you'll be amazed at how they'll respond to you and your ministry.

- *Kids' learning styles are rewired.* I believe this is the most evident area that kids' brains have been rewired. Technology and media have brought significant changes in the way kids learn and how we effectively communicate to them. Parents also recognize this. Technology and media have become more than entertainment. Parents actually find the educational value of media incredibly helpful. Teachers use many different types of technology in classrooms, from editing video content, to laptop computing, to podcasting.

- *Technology and media have moved children from verbal to visual learners.* They're the generation that hears with their eyes. Images are the information vehicle for Generation M. Whereas previous generations focused on words, this generation focuses on images. DVDs and video games far outsell books today.

  How can we effectively minister to them? Speak their language...use visual communication. Speak to them with screens and monitors. Many churches are now moving to video-based curricula with great effectiveness. Why? They're sharing God's truth in the language of Generation M, and they're listening and retaining—with their eyes. Bible verses are just as powerful on a screen as on a page. Same words—just written on a different type of material. A picture truly is worth a thousand words to today's kids.

- *Technology and media have shortened children's attention spans.* Rapid visual change is the norm for them. A Web site has only a few seconds to load, or children impatiently move to another site. It seems almost painful for kids to wait for a video game disk to load. Sesame Street recognized this abbreviated attention span, so it programmed its show segments to last only four minutes or less. Surf over to any children's TV network and you'll find images moving nonstop.

How can we effectively minister to them? Work *with* the speed of kids' attention, not against it. Don't expect kids to act like little adults. Deliver your lessons at the dynamic speed in which they thrive best. Yes, there are times when we need to teach kids to slow down, be still, and know that he is God. But if your primary ministry speed is pedestrian, you won't effectively connect with today's kids.

It's OK to teach children that they can connect with Jesus not only in the stillness of the wilderness but also in the busyness of the marketplace. We've all been trapped listening to a robotic, mind-numbing lecture, and it's not something that'll draw kids clamoring to your church. In *The Tipping Point*, author Malcolm Gladwell pointed out that kids watch when they understand and look away when they are bored. We need to see what they are watching and what they are not watching. Ask yourself the hard question: Have you dared to deliver through *their* eyes?

- *Technology and media have produced information overload.* By 2002, according to Media Dynamics, Inc., the average American was exposed to about 250 different commercials in a day—up nearly 25 percent since the mid-1970s. Kids can do an Internet search for a word or phrase and gain unlimited information on any subject. So much information is thrust at today's kids that it's a challenge to get any one message to stick. The clutter of so many messages does present a challenge. How do you get any one message to stick with Generation M? Will they remember your lesson from even a week ago? After all, they've been bombarded with hundreds of commercials and e-mails since then.

How can we effectively minister to them? Consider teaching fewer truths. Decide what kids *must* know for their particular stage in life, and repeat those truths over and over and over again. The children's ministry at my church has narrowed its teaching truths down to one a month, and each year we repeat those same truths. The result? Kids remember the truths we taught them months and months ago. The same thing applies to Bible memory. I believe it's more effective for kids to learn one verse each month than to be presented with a new verse each week. "Stickiness" means a message makes an impact. You can't get it out of your head—it sticks in your memory. Give Generation M Bible truths that stick by teaching what's essential.

- *Technology and media have produced an experience-based generation.* Kids flock to experience theme parks like Universal Studios and restaurants like the Rainforest Cafe. They seek to be entertained, thrilled, and engaged in an adventure. Many educators and marketers have learned to communicate their information through these venues. "Edutainment" has emerged as an effective way to reach Generation M. Edutainment is the act of learning through a medium that both educates and amuses.

Educators agree that kids learn best when they're excited by what they're learning. Unfortunately, that can't happen unless the material is served up in an exciting and entertaining way. According to Leonard Sweet, author of *Carpe Mañana*, today's generation's learning is "eye popping, ear ringing, nose tingling, mouth watering, finger-licking learning."

How can we effectively minister to them? Study the strategies developed by theme parks, restaurants, and entertainment centers. Theme out your children's environments and create an experience. No matter what your budget is, with a little creativity you can create a fresh, engaging experience for the children in your area. God called me a year ago to start over—to get out of my comfort zone and move across the country to another church—to lead them into an experience-based, edutainment model of children's ministry. The change has been amazing as we've shifted to connect with Generation M. Our attendance has grown by 45 percent, and we can attribute most of that growth to unchurched kids in our area. Our first- through third-grade environment is aptly named "The Fun Factory… Where God Makes Church Fun!" We want kids to experience God in a fun, relevant, engaging way.

- *Technology and media have fueled interactive learning.* Today's kids want to have a part in the learning process as well as the outcome. The hit TV show *American Idol* is an example of this, with millions of people voting to determine the winner. Web sites are finding ways to let kids have a say in their material instead of merely pushing content at them. The *Kids' Choice Awards* are a huge hit with kids as they decide which actors and movies to award.

How can we effectively minister to them? Give kids choices while teaching. Let them be active learners involved in the leaning process instead of passive listeners.

- *Kids' families are being rewired.* Technology has become a part of families' daily lives. TV, DVDs, or the Internet are activities that kids can enjoy while parents are talking. Stressed-out parents plug in *Shrek* so they have reprieve for an hour and a half. In some cases, technology is used as a bonding tool between parent and child through video games or movies. But it can also squeeze out family time as each family member retreats to his or her own bedroom or area to watch TV or surf the Web. Many parents also use technology and media as a discipline tool—either as a reward or a punishment. Technology and media are even used as tools to change kids' behavior when they're grouchy, hyper, or fighting. Technology and media are constant companions that are rarely turned off.

  How can we effectively minister to them? Encourage families to turn the TV off during meals—and simply talk. Provide Internet safety classes for parents so they can guide their children on the Web. Provide devotional tools for families. Set up a family ministry Web site and provide online parenting resources for parents. Record your lessons and place them on the Web site so parents can see and hear what their child is learning. Provide discussion questions that go along with the online lesson. There are many ways you can impact families in a positive way with technology and media.

- *Kids' relationships with others are being rewired.* The Internet is supposed to be about connecting people. But it can actually create a distance between people. Face-to-face conversations are easily replaced with virtual reality.

  How can we effectively minister to them? Make a strong commitment to have personal, face-to-face relationships. Great environments, facilities, and programming will get kids into the doors of your ministry, but personal relationships will produce a life change and keep them.

- *Kids' relationship with God is being rewired.* Technology and media can become idols that kids prioritize before their relationship with God. After hours and hours in front of the screen or monitor, there's simply no time left to spend with God. Kids can also be exposed to harmful influences on the Web that can lead them down dangerous paths away from the truth.

How can we effectively minister to them? Teach kids to spend quiet time with God each day away from technology and media. Encourage parents to closely monitor their child's Internet surfing and to place safety blocks on the computer to protect the child. Teach kids to avoid harmful sites and to guard their eyes against sin.

IT'S TIME TO REWIRE OUR MINISTRY

Churches and ministries are traveling on dirt back roads while the generation we're trying to reach is speeding along on the information superhighway. We can try to ignore it and keep doing what we've always done, but the results of denial will become more and more apparent as kids fall away from stale ministries. We can't reach empty seats. Secular companies like McDonald's seem to understand this concept better than most churches. Their food remains constant but the kid's meal toy and branding follow cultural relevance. We, the church, would do well to take notice of this principle if we're going to reach Generation M. Our "food" will always stay the same, but the way we present it must change with the culture if we're to be tasted by this generation.

I'll never forget my son standing there that Christmas morning, holding the old, ungainly cell phone.

"This is *not* a cell phone," he said.

It was true. To his generation, it was not a cell phone. We must ask ourselves this question: Is Generation M holding our ministry out at arm's length, saying, "This is *not* a ministry that's relevant to my life. I can't use this!"

As I type this, I'm looking out my window at the Las Vegas strip. The bright lights of one of the world's entertainment capitals fill the skyline. Thousands of people are being entertained in some of the most elaborate buildings and shows in the world. The technology and media powering all this are incredible. The excitement in the air will persist until late, late into the night. But it's all about making money, an earthly treasure that will not last forever.

This weekend, technology and media will be used somewhere else in Las Vegas: in a children's environment at a church. Kids of Generation M will flood through the doors. Technology and media will not be used to make money; rather, they'll be used as tools to share God's eternal truth. Can you imagine the results? They'll be far more valuable than any jackpot at the casino. In fact, they'll be priceless. As God uses the technology and media he's provided for us to communicate his Word, the result will be changed lives.

The comfort zone of outdated ministry is no longer valid—the answer lies somewhere on the edge. Are you willing to reach for it?

Try This

BY STEVE PAROLINI

Activity 1

CHURCH AS A VIDEO GAME

Uh-oh…we're about to give kids the remote! They'll apply Acts 20:28 to their own view of their church as they turn a typical Sunday morning into a "video game."

Before the lesson, clear a space in your meeting room. If convenient, collect a few video game controllers (standard remote control devices would work just as well).

Explain to the children that they're going to be characters in a life-size video game. Choose two people who will be the Players, and then assign roles similar to the following to the rest of the children: pastor, offering collector, choir director, choir members (one or more), congregation (one or more). If your church features other roles, assign children these as well. Tailor this to your own church tradition.

Have all the children except for the two Players arrange themselves as if they're in an actual church service. Help as necessary, but allow the kids to determine what that looks like. Have the Players stand next to each other facing the rest of the group. Then give the Players each a video game controller and say: **As the Players, your job is to control the rest of the kids as if they're in a video game called "Our Church on a Sunday Morning." You'll take turns calling out instructions for different characters to act out as you play the game.**

You might want to suggest some actions the Players can call out, such as: "Pastor, give a sermon" or "Offering collector, take the offering," but allow children their own creativity in giving instructions. Encourage them to be as accurate to a real service or as silly as they want.

Several times during the game, call "pause," and have everyone freeze. At this time, change players' roles so that everyone gets a chance to be a few different characters in the video game church.

As the leader, you reserve the right to call "restart" if things get a bit out of hand. In that case, everyone will return to their starting positions.

After playing for a while, "turn off" the video game and discuss the experience. Ask:

- **How is this video game like a real church service? How is it different?**
- **What did you like about a video game based on church? What didn't you like?**

- If you were in charge of the actual service, how would you change it? What would the buttons on your controller do?
- In this game (and in many video games) there was a pause button. Are there times you'd like to "pause" your life? When? Why?
- We also had a "reset" button in this game. Are there times when you wish life had a reset button? Explain.

Activity 2

CELL PHONE

For this activity, you'll need two cell phones. Program the numbers for each into the other to make the game easier.

Have kids form two groups. Give a cell phone to each group and have one of the groups go to a different room. (If it's a nice day, have one go outside while the other remains in the classroom.)

In each group, have kids decide who will go first. Join one of the groups, and have the first volunteer in that group follow you a short distance from the others so no one will hear your conversation. Then whisper to that person the following sentence: "There are lots of ways to show Jesus' love to others, and calling your friends just to tell them you care is one way." Then have that child call the other cell phone (the first person in that group should be holding the phone and will move away from his or her group to answer it) and repeat the sentence. When the other child hears the sentence, he or she is to hang up, then call the first cell phone back and repeat the sentence to the next person who answers in that group. Alternate between groups until all have had a turn. It's important that those on the phone at any given time can't be heard by the rest of their group. You'll need the assistance of another volunteer to make sure of this in the other group's location.

Once the final call has been received, have the person who answered the phone repeat the phrase to you (be sure to write down what you hear). Then have everyone form a large group and read the original sentence aloud, comparing it to the final sentence. Ask:
- **Would it have been easier or harder to remember this sentence if you were talking face-to-face with the other person? Why?**
- **Why do you think cell phones are so popular? How are they helpful? In what ways might they not be helpful?**
- **Why is it important to make sure people understand what you're saying?**
- **If Jesus called you on your cell phone, would your conversation with him sound different from your conversation with your friends? How?**
- **What are some ways to make sure a friend understands what you're saying?**

Say: **It's important to make sure we're understood when we are talking to others, especially if we're talking about something as important as Jesus' love. This week, make your conversations count. Treat your calls as though Jesus is on the other end, and be sure you're saying what you mean to say.**

Activity 3

RUNNING THE SHOW

Apply 1 Timothy 4:12-14 to your kids' *roles* in your church services. You'll need the cooperation of church leaders who work with the technologies utilized during the Sunday service (computers, lights, sound system, video screens, etc.). Each week, for a month or two, have a few children join the person running sound or lights or the computer (or whatever) to observe and, when appropriate, help out in running the church service. To make this a good experience, talk with the people who run those technologies ahead of time, and ask them to welcome the children as either observers or helpers (whichever is more comfortable or practical). For example, if a headset is used to communicate instructions, have one of the children listen in to see what goes on behind the scenes. Or have a child push the "start" button on a tape recorder.

If your church is decidedly "low-tech" in its church worship service, you might have children work instead with the technologies you use in church school classes (microphones, overhead projectors, etc.).

After their week assisting the running of the church service, have children report on their experience. Ask:

- **What did you learn about the church service?**
- **What was it like to be a part of the team that runs the service?**
- **What surprised you most?**
- **What effect does technology have on the service?**
- **What are the good things that technology does for church? What are some things that might not be so good?**
- **What role would you like to have someday to help run a church service?**

Activity 4

DISTRACTIONS

Proverbs 4:25-27 is all about focus. It encourages us to stay the course, fix on what's important—but kids today are bombarded with distractions that make this difficult. Use this activity to help kids discover where distractions might come from and what they can do to focus on what's relevant.

Meet in a room that can accommodate a variety of competing technologies. For instance, you'll want to hook up a TV and any type of sound system (or portable boombox), then add as many other distractions as you can such as computers, video games…whatever you can dig up. If kids have cell phones or portable video games, ask them to bring these.

Open the activity in silence. Invite the children to look up Proverbs 4:25-27 with a partner and read it aloud. Then, before doing anything else, turn on all of the distractions, encouraging children to talk on their cell phones or play their video games and otherwise just be completely enveloped in the sound and images.

When things are rolling at full speed, start a discussion using the following questions. You'll likely find it difficult to get responses, but keep at it—try to get kids to think about the Scripture passage. In the midst of commotion, ask:

- **What do you think the writer of this psalm was trying to say?**
- **What do you think it means to "mark out a straight path"?**
- **What are ways we get sidetracked?**

After attempting a discussion for a time, slowly remove the distractions until kids are no longer bombarded by noise and images. Use whatever method you normally do to resume quiet, and have kids sit with their eyes closed for a few seconds until the room is peaceful. Then have them open their eyes, and calmly ask:

- **What was it like to talk about this Bible passage with all of the distractions?**
- **Were you able to concentrate? Why or why not?**
- **What does this tell us about how technology can help us or get in the way?**

Read the Scripture passage again, and repeat the initial discussion questions. Encourage children to take time away from distractions now and then so they can spend quiet time with God.

Activity 5

THE ART OF UNITY

Ephesians 4:2-3 is a great reminder of our calling to cooperate with each other for God's greater good. Guide kids toward a spirit of teamwork as they learn more about each other and discover ways they can collaborate for God.

For this activity, you'll need an overhead projector and sheets of opaque paper (dark construction paper works well). Form groups of no more than five, and give each group a supply of paper.

Have group members tear paper into shapes that represent something about themselves. For example, a child might tear a football shape to express an interest in playing football. Or someone might tear a star shape because he or she wants to be a movie star someday. Allow children plenty of time to tear one or more shapes. Have children explain the meaning of their shapes to other members of their small group.

Then have each small group come up with a way to combine the shapes into one silhouette that represents the group collectively. In other words, kids might link or overlap their shapes to form a cross (representing their shared faith) or a big pizza (representing their shared love for food).

One group at a time, have kids come to the front of the room and arrange their pieces into the group's unified shape on the overhead. The image will be projected as a silhouette for everyone to see. Allow other groups to guess what the individual shapes and the unifying shape represent, then have the presenting group explain or clarify as necessary.

When all groups have presented, ask:

- **What did you discover about members of your group that you didn't know before?**
- **How did your group decide what to choose as the unifying shape?**

Read Ephesians 4:2-3 aloud. Ask:

- **In what ways did we express unity in this activity?**
- **How can similar interests bring us together? In what ways does technology bring us together?**

Bonus Idea: If your church has access to a computer that can project onto a screen, you can add high-tech flair by having kids take turns drawing shapes in a simple paint program on the computer. Then have them arrange those shapes around the screen to form their unifying shapes. You'll want to test the paint program ahead of time to make sure it's easy for kids to use.

Activity 6

ENCOURAGING E-MAIL

Paul was a wonderful encourager to believers, and your kids can learn to encourage, too.

For this activity you'll need paper and pens or pencils. Form groups of no more than four and distribute paper and pens or pencils to each group. Read aloud Acts 20:1-2, then say: **Paul was a great teacher but also a great encourager to others. We're going to do some encouraging of our own today. Paul didn't have e-mail or the Internet to pass along his words, but we do! Today let's use "e-mail" to encourage each other.**

Have kids work in their groups to come up with e-mail "addresses" for each group member. Explain that these e-mail addresses need to be uplifting, positive, and encouraging. For example, someone might get the e-mail address greatartist@friend.com or funfriend@laughter.com. Wander around the groups and help as needed, encouraging creativity and reminding kids that these are invented names.

Once everyone has an e-mail address, have each person write their e-mail address on the top of a sheet of paper and tape the paper to a wall. These will be "computer screens." Leave space between each one so kids can approach the screens and write on them. Then give kids time to write brief e-mail messages (or simply draw pictures) to each other on the screens. Make sure they "sign" their e-mail messages with their own e-mail address. Remind kids to be encouraging and positive with their words and pictures. To make sure everyone gets a similar number of messages, ask kids to write something on each screen, or assign a certain number of screens to each small group.

Add your own messages. (You did choose an e-mail address, didn't you?) Then ask:

- **How did you feel about helping decide on an e-mail address for your group members? for yourself?**
- **What was it like to be encouraged with other people's e-mail messages?**
- **How can we encourage each other throughout this month?**

Say: **E-mail is a great way to communicate with each other. Let's remember to be like Paul as he traveled from city to city. Make it your goal to say positive things often in your e-mail and to be an encourager.**

Activity 7

THE FAMILY SHOW

The Bible is timeless. Proverbs 17:17 exhorts friends to help friends and brothers to help each other, and that loyalty is just as necessary today as it was long ago. How have creature comforts affected the way we relate to one another? How has technology impacted the way we respond to biblical truths? Explore these questions with your kids as they act out a day in the life of a family without today's gadgets. Observe the contrast when they approach the same scenario *with* our life-changing gadgets.

Form groups of no more than five. Have groups each choose a popular TV show that features a family—each group member will assume the role of one of the characters from that show.

Say: **Family life is different today than it was 50 years ago. I'm going to give you a scene to act out with your group. The first time you act it out, I want you to go back in time—pretend there are no computers, no video games, no cell phones, no television sets, and if you have a regular phone, it's not working. In fact, NO electronics are working except the lights in your house! The second time, I want you to act out the same scene as if it were happening today with all the technology you have at home.**

Assign either of the following scenes to each group:
- Family members are trying to decide what to do on a snowy day when they can't go out to friends' houses or anywhere else. Your parents want you to play with your brother and sister, who are bored and cranky.
- Children in the family are planning a big all-night party with friends, and they want to invite their friends to the party right away. The parents want to know what they can do to help prepare for the party.

Mingle with the groups and assist as necessary, helping kids act out the first run-through (without technology) and the second (with technology). If you have lots of time, groups can perform their skits for the rest of the group.

Prompt kids with these considerations in their role-plays:

- **What would "fun" look like to someone who didn't have a computer or a video game system or a phone?**
- **How would you get in touch with friends to tell them about a party if you didn't have the Internet or phones?**
- **How can kids and their parents work together to figure out things to do?**

After the role-plays, have children sit and discuss the following questions:

- **What surprised you about your first skit compared to your second skit?**
- **Did technology make any difference in the way you treated your family or your friends?**
- **What's something good that technology has given to families? What's something it might have taken away?**

Activity 8

HOW WOULD YOU TEACH THAT?

Let kids be the leaders in this activity that allows them to teach an entire lesson.

Form three groups. Each group will be given the task of creating a plan for teaching the message of Romans 8:39, which tells us that nothing can separate us from God's love. The groups won't have to actually prepare the lesson—they'll just come up with a plan for how they'd run it according to their assigned method. Ask them to demonstrate or explain their plan for the rest of the group.

Here are the three groups and a note or two about each:

- Words only/no technology allowed: This group must come up with a way to teach the message without using any technology at all—just through spoken words.
- High-tech only: This group must use at least three kinds of technology to present its lesson (computers, phones, televisions, video…whatever they choose). However, they can't rely on any traditional methods (no discussions, no teacher-led presentation, etc.). Only technology.
- Whatever works: This group can use anything they like to present the message: discussion, technology, role-playing, and so on.

Encourage groups to brainstorm creative ways to teach the message from Romans 8:39 that nothing can separate us from God. Some groups might want paper and pencils to make notes or draw up their plan.

When groups are ready, have them present their idea to the rest of the class. Give kudos to all the ideas, then discuss the following:

- **What was it like to come up with a plan using the rules I gave you?**
- **How can technology help teach a message? Which method do you think you'd like the best? Why?**
- **What are some of the best things you've learned in school? How did you learn those things?**

Say: **It's true that nothing can separate us from God's love. That's a pretty important message! But each of us might learn that lesson in a different way. It's not as important *how* we learn as it is *what* we learn. Let's ask God to help us look for ways to learn in all situations.**

Activity 9

LESSONS FROM MOVIES

The idea of this activity is to show children how they can learn biblical truth even from movies and other entertainment. Just as Jesus used stories to teach, so can you! You'll need a TV and VCR or DVD player along with copies of movies to show clips from.

Tip

Copyright Laws—Movie clips under three minutes are technically covered under the fair use doctrine (which allows portions of a work to be exhibited for educational purposes). But to be on the safe side, you can obtain a license for a small fee from Christian Video Licensing International. Visit www.cvli.org for more information. (You can't charge admission to a function where you screen clips.)

Here are a few examples of video clips that could prompt lots of discussion on a variety of topics. Keep an eye out for popular children-friendly films, and you'll discover a wealth of content to use in your classroom.

A few suggestions:
- In the movie *Hook*, Peter Banning (a grown-up Peter Pan) perplexes the Lost Boys because they don't believe he's really Peter Pan. But when one Lost Boy stretches Peter's face into a smile, he recognizes him and says, "There you are, Peter." The discussion for this clip could be about how sometimes we don't think we're the people we should be (when we mess up, when we feel alone or lost), but that God can always see the smile he put in us—the person he made us to be. *Jeremiah 1:5*
- There are a number of scenes in the animated film *Chicken Little* that illustrate the idea of trust. Choose one or more and show them to children to spark a discussion about what it means to be trustworthy and how important it is to always tell the truth. *Colossians 3:9*

- Show the scene from *Napoleon Dynamite* where Napoleon decides to go onstage and take care of Pedro's "talent" portion of the assembly with his dance. This is one of many great scenes in this movie that show what friendship looks like. It's a great discussion starter about "what would you do to help a friend?" *John 15:13*

In addition to the actual video excerpt and related discussion, use this time to help children see that stories are a great way to learn about God and how to be Christ-like. Explain that some movies and TV shows illustrate how not to live, while others show us how to live.

Read Mark 4:2a aloud. Ask:

- **Why do you think Jesus used stories to teach his message?**
- **How can we learn from stories today?**
- **If you could tell Jesus a story about your faith, what would you tell him?**

Have kids think of scenes from their favorite movies that teach a good point, then invite them to share those with the rest of the class.

Activity 10

SPECIAL EFFECTS

"He does great things too marvelous to understand. He performs countless miracles" (Job 5:9).

Hollywood doesn't hold a candle to the amazing scenes God creates. Kids will get a better idea of God's might when they compare "the real thing" with movie special effects.

For this activity, you'll need a few movie clips from recent films that include sensational special effects. Think of natural disasters, enormous bugs…you get the idea. Choose nearly any scene from *The Chronicles of Narnia: The Lion, the Witch and the Wardrobe*. It won't be difficult to find a scene that illustrates Hollywood's ability to create a thrilling effect using innovation and computer graphics and camera trickery.

Begin the activity by showing the clips to the kids. Then ask them to explain how they know these aren't actual events. Invite kids to describe their favorite "special effects" scene from a movie or TV show they've seen. Ask:

- **What is it about these amazing things that tell you they're not real?**
- **How do you know what's real and what's a special effect?**
- **If you could create a special effect right now, what would you choose?**

Then ask children to recall their favorite miraculous story from the Bible. Here are a few to get things started:

- Moses parts the Red Sea (Exodus 14:21-22)
- Jonah is swallowed by a fish but not consumed (Jonah 1:17)
- Jesus feeds 5,000 people with just a few loaves and fish (Mark 6:41-44)
- Jesus walks on water (John 6:19)

Ask:

- **What is the difference between a miracle and a special effect?**
- **What does a miracle say about God's power? What do special effects say about man's power?**
- **Imagine actually witnessing a miracle from the Bible. How do you think you would've reacted? How is that the same as or different from the way you react to a special effect in a movie?**

Say: **Today people can make just about anything look real using computers—but only God can perform true miracles.**

Hottest Educational Trends

WHAT'S NEW
(RELATIVELY SPEAKING)

BY HEATHER DUNN

The word *hot* is used today to mean everything from the opposite of cold to attractive to trendy. In this chapter we'll consider educational practices that are hottest—not cold, not trendy, and not outdated. They may not represent brand-new concepts, but they're the most popular schools of thought today. And they all claim to help children learn and internalize their learning more effectively. Here's an array of philosophies, not just one idea. Allow these learning theories to stimulate your thinking, stretch your imagination, and perhaps even spark new ideas that you could apply to your ministry to reach even more children for Jesus.

Why should children's ministers be concerned about educational trends? First of all, our children are experiencing these techniques in schools today.

Second, if there is solid research about how children learn, can we use that information to make wise choices and apply it appropriately to our classes?

Third, we need to keep up with our changing world. The American Society of Training and Documentation reported that the total body of knowledge is increasing at an incredible rate; it has doubled in the past decade and is doubling again every 18 months. Staying as current as possible helps us stay relevant as we teach our kids. Schools no longer focus on a single body of facts. On which ones would they focus? We need to consider this thinking with our lessons, too.

And a fourth reason is that technology is changing rapidly and allowing our children to have instant access to all kinds of data that their grandparents had to commit to memory. Technology also enables our children to see and hear things that their grandparents (and even parents) had to imagine. Kids today are used to listening to music, texting their friends, and working on homework all at the same time. They think more globally because they can just as easily text a missionary child on the other side of the world as they can their next-door neighbor. They can see real video of wars, tornadoes, and the blood coursing through their bodies all within minutes on their personal computer screen. How in the world can anyone effectively teach these children? It's not an easy task, and the answer doesn't lie in one easy method. Let's look at some of the options.

MULTIPLE INTELLIGENCES

First proposed by educational theorist Howard Gardner, the theory of multiple intelligences suggests that there are many ways in which we synthesize or digest information. He also proposed that each person employs a unique blend of these intelligences as he or she learns. The number of intelligences now included in the list varies from seven to more than 10.

What *are* the multiple intelligences?

- **Word Smart:** Those with the verbal/linguistic intelligence prefer to use language in all of its forms to learn. They are often able to learn new languages easily. They enjoy expressing themselves through written or spoken words.
- **Logic Smart:** Some people specialize in logical/mathematical processing. They lean toward mathematical problem solving, logic, and scientific investigations.
- **Music Smart:** Others prefer musical/rhythmic processing. They are predisposed to recognizing rhythms, tones, and musical patterns as well as composing them.
- **Body Smart:** There are those who prefer bodily/kinesthetic learning. They get their whole body into the learning, often in the forms of sports, creating objects, dance, or drama.
- **Picture Smart:** Those with spatial/visual intelligence see things in three dimensions and patterns most easily. Someone with interpersonal abilities prefers to look at things from the point of view of other's intentions, motivations, and desires.

- **People Smart:** Intrapersonal processors have a keener awareness of themselves and use that understanding to learn about the world around them.
- **Nature Smart:** The naturalist most readily relates to living things and the systems of which they are a part.
  (In addition to these, spiritual intelligence, existential intelligence, and moral intelligence are also occasionally included as unique and viable learning preferences.)

Anyone reading this list will naturally identify with several of these intelligences and identify others they know who fit the descriptions of the rest. It's easy to see that any classroom could contain children who fall into each of these categories. This means that if you want to reach as many children as possible so they can know and understand the love of God through Jesus, you need to incorporate learning opportunities using each of these intelligences. It may not be possible to incorporate all the intelligences every week, but addressing different ones each week will draw in different kinds of learners and provide opportunities for a significant number of children to be learning optimally.

How do I know which intelligences are present in my classroom? As you look at your lessons, try to identify the intelligences that are being used. When children are writing, you'll engage the children with verbal/linguistic. When they're role-playing, you'll involve children with bodily/kinesthetic. If the class is singing, you'll capture the children with the musical/rhythmic intelligence. Asking children to tell the story of Zacchaeus from Zacchaeus' point of view especially appeals to those with intrapersonal abilities. If you want to learn how the children in your church learn, try different kinds of activities like these and watch to see which ones the children become the most involved in.

Questions to Ponder

- Which intelligences can I address in my classes that I haven't before?
- How can I remember to consistently address the learning needs of my children who think differently from me?
- How can I better understand my children who process and learn differently from me?

BRAIN-BASED LEARNING

Brain-based learning is a theory based on how the brain receives and processes information. (If you're a logical/mathematical processor, you'll be interested in reading the scientific explanation for this!) In layman's terms, this theory asserts that the brain learns naturally and can perform several activities at once. The information the brain receives is stored in many places, and no two brains organize information exactly the same way. This theory also says that our brains develop better by interacting with other brains, meaning our learning is enhanced in small interactive groups. The brain retrieves stored information through multiple pathways.

Brain-based theorists also believe that emotion is extremely important to patterning—and patterning is how the brain determines meaning. Because of this, emotions play a significant role in how our brain pays attention, puts meaning to information, and remembers. This theory also concludes that complex learning is enhanced by challenge and inhibited by stress.

As a result of these ideas, two applications have emerged. The three-tiered brain-based application includes orchestrated immersion (creating learning environments that allow students to experience as many aspects of learning as possible), relaxed alertness (no worries, but lots of thinking), and active processing (letting children actively process together to consolidate and internalize what they've learned).

Differentiated instruction has also grown from this research. Teachers using differentiated instruction allow children at different stages of learning or with different learning styles to learn at their own pace or using their own strengths. Teachers incorporate learning styles and the classroom environment into the planning of lessons. They also encourage students to move at their own pace and through activities that enable them to learn most effectively.

So what does this type of instruction look like in action? Modern classrooms based on either brain-based or differentiated instruction include spaces for small groups of children to interact. Children have options, often with several varied activities going on at once. There could be music playing, water gurgling, smells wafting, objects to touch, and visual displays. Teachers ask the children to talk about their feelings and how they're processing what they've experienced.

What would this look like in a Sunday school classroom? Much like the modern classroom described above. According to the brain-based research, the perfect Sunday school lesson would be free from stress (dimmed lights, soothing fragrances, quality music in the background) yet challenging (children thinking through problems and situations). Classrooms would be environments where students taste, smell, touch, and hear things that relate to the lesson. The lesson would include children interacting with each other by processing together what they are learning (they work in small groups or teams). The lessons would also include a variety of learning places (large groups, small groups, art, music, quiet introspection, role-plays, computers, and reading). At least some of these activities would be available for students as they choose. And the perfect lesson would make an emotional connection with the learning.

Again, it wouldn't be practical to provide all of this every Sunday, but incorporating a relevant smell or a taste each week could be fun, and playing background music would add dimension. Considering all the options requires planning, but the payoff is too large to ignore. Test each idea by asking yourself this: Would it open learning pathways in children's minds that would allow them to seek and to find an eternal relationship with Jesus?

Questions to Ponder

- How can I offer my children the opportunity to think seriously about what they are learning?
- In what different ways are my children experiencing the lesson?
- Are my children talking to each other about what they are learning?
- In what ways are my children making an emotional connection to the lessons?

COLLABORATIVE LEARNING

Collaborative learning is known by several other names—cooperative learning, peer coaching, team-based learning, or interactive learning—and carries a variety of meanings in education today. For the most part, collaborative learning means that children are learning in small non-competitive groups. These small groups range in size from two to no more than six. Most often these groups contain a range of ages or ability levels. Sometimes the teacher assigns the students to groups, while other times students choose the group. Sometimes groups are informal groups that form for a short period of time to discuss questions or to try an interesting experiment. Other times the groups are more formal, working on the same project over a number of days. Long-term groups give students the opportunity to stay together—several months, a year, or even more—and learn many things together.

Each type of group has its own merit. The challenge is to design meaningful work for groups to do that requires all members to actively engage. Teachers using collaborative learning work hard to ensure age-level appropriateness, to provide clear instructions, and to include a division of labor that equitably enlists all of the children.

What's the benefit for a Sunday school classroom? A collaborative environment would allow children to work in small groups for a significant amount of time. Today, we call this the large group/small group approach. The small groups can range from multi-age groups to specialized groups of children based on age and gender. It's a flexible model—children could rotate to a new group each week, or they could remain in the same group for a year or more. The basics of the lesson may be presented to the whole group, while digging into the Bible and making life applications is done in the small groups.

Questions to Ponder

- When can I best use small groups for children to learn as well as synthesize what they've learned?
- How can I prepare my children to work effectively in their small group experience—and get the most out of it?

THE 3 R'S

The Bill and Melinda Gates Foundation pours millions of dollars into schools willing to use the "3 R's": rigor, relevance, and relationships. Why such generous contributions? Because the foundation strongly believes that students learn best in small groups that focus on these three key components. The foundation suggests that students should be challenged to dig deep and think hard. It stresses that lessons should be interesting because they relate to daily life. And it recognizes that all kids need someone who will mentor and encourage them. Though the Gates Foundation currently focuses primarily on high school students, it's included here because it won't be long before it applies to younger students as well. We'll be a step ahead if we consider the implications this has for us in the church.

What would a 3 R's Sunday school classroom look like? Children would be asked "thinking" questions—no one-word answers. They would be asked to explain and defend their thinking. Children would leave their classes ready and anxious to apply what they've learned about God in their daily lives. Children would know one caring adult who expects to see them every Sunday and who expects to hear how they're growing in their faith.

Questions to Ponder

- How am I asking my kids to think seriously about their faith?
- How am I ensuring that all children see a way to apply their learning to their daily lives?
- How can I provide for mentoring relationships for my children?

EDUCATIONALLY, WHAT WON'T CHANGE?

In spite of emerging trends, there will always be certain constants in the realm of education. For instance, you'll never find any two identical children. They'll always come from a variety of backgrounds. They'll have lived in different places, experienced life in different ways, eaten different foods, and played different games. God didn't create any two of them alike. Neither are their parents, siblings, grandparents, aunts, uncles, cousins, or friends exactly alike. You'll never have any two children who are the same!

R.E.A.L. Learning

Group Publishing has developed easy guidelines for determining which activities will help kids learn best and which won't. It's called *R.E.A.L. Learning.* R.E.A.L. Learning is **relational,** relying on learner-to-learner interaction to enhance learning and build friendships. It's **experiential**—what learners experience will stick with them up to nine times longer. It's also **applicable.** Kids are challenged to find how the experience or truth applies to their own personal, day-to-day lives. And, last, it's **learner-based** because kids learn best when the learning process takes into consideration how they learn best.

Children will always learn best through a myriad of tactics. What works for one child won't work for another. One will prefer music, another will prefer art, and the next will prefer role-plays. One will want to see it, the next will want to hear it, most will want to do it. This will never change. There will never be one best way to reach all children. So, the bigger your bag of tricks and the more you know about educational practices, the better able you'll be to reach children with the life-transforming knowledge of Jesus. You'll have more ways to reach more kids. God doesn't speak to any of us in the same way. He'd probably like it if we took after him in this regard!

There will always be a variety of things that affect learning. Children as well as adults are affected by what happens around them. When life is rough, it's hard to concentrate on learning new things. When kids are fighting with their friends, worried about their safety, or dealing with death (even if the deceased is their goldfish), they're distracted. They may not remember the point of your lesson last week—unless, of course, it relates directly to their problem. But they *can* learn that you care and that God cares. Don't despair if their problems or worries interfere with their learning a predefined lesson. Look at it this way: These same issues may pave the way for very deep learning if we take the time to delve into the world of a hurting or worried child.

Kids will still be kids. Their curiosity will never change. Hide something under a sheet, set out an odd collection of items, tell kids not to touch something, and what happens? They look, touch, experiment. Children are naturally inquisitive. Pique your children's curiosity, and you've got them hooked. Anticipate their curiosity and you won't be upset when they peek or taste or rearrange. Embrace their curiosity and you'll have lots of fun!

Best of all, the importance of our subject matter will never change! We have the most amazing, relevant, helpful, unchanging, hope-filling, life-changing subject in the world. No one anywhere has anything more important to tell the world than we do. Every lesson, story, and Scripture is packed with life application. Children need to know God's unconditional love for them through Jesus. We are blessed to have the timeless message of God's love and truth. God promises to be with us, help us, and strengthen us. God never changes and neither do his promises. Although everything else will change, God never will.

Questions to Ponder

• How can I use these "unchangeables" to my best advantage with my children?
• What are other constants I can rely on?

SO WHAT DOES ALL THIS MEAN FOR THE CHURCH?

What does all this suggest for you and me in children's ministry today? next year? 10 years from now? It means we need to keep learning. We cannot become lazy or complacent. We need to become experts about new ideas, about what kids are like, about how kids learn. If we stop growing, so will our children. This also means that we need to be excellent. God deserves our excellence, and so do our children. And if any subject matter needs to be presented in the most excellent way, it's ours.

Of course, this might mean you'll need to educate those around you to gain their support. It might mean you'll want to change the way you run your classrooms. It might even mean your kids will be more involved in aspects of your church where they never set foot before.

But God has entrusted us with his children. Because of this, we need to make sure we'll reach each child with the good news of Jesus when we choose teaching materials and lessons. And when we do, God will be there to finish what we've begun.

Final Questions to Ponder

- How might God feel about the learning environments I've created in my church?
- If Jesus were observing my class, what would I do differently?

RESOURCES FOR FURTHER STUDY

Gardner, Howard, *Frames of Mind: The Theory of Multiple Intelligences*. New York, NY: BasicBooks, 1983.

Jensen, Eric, *Teaching With the Brain in Mind*. Alexandria, VA: Association for Supervision and Curriculum Development, 1998.

Kotulak, Ronald, *Inside the Brain: Revolutionary Discoveries of How the Mind Works*. Kansas City, MO: Andrews McMeel Publishing, 1996.

Sousa, David A., *How the Brain Learns*. Thousand Oaks, CA: Corwin Press, 2006.

Try This

BY SCOTT KINNER

FAITH STORY STATIONS

By tapping into multiple intelligences, this activity will help kids discover how they've grown in their faith—and *you'll* gain insight into their spiritual growth as well.

Set up four Faith Story Stations:

• At the first station, prepare a CD player with quiet, reflective music. Set out paper and pencils for kids to write a song.

• At the second station, arrange comfortable chairs or pillows where kids can sit and talk.

• At the third station, set out several kinds of art supplies, such as canvas and paint, paper and pencils, modeling clay, and craft supplies.

• At the fourth station, set out blank white paper, construction paper, a stapler, pencils, and colored pencils for kids to create a book.

Say: **Think about the first time you ever heard about Jesus. It might've been in Sunday school, or maybe a friend or a parent talked to you. Or maybe you can't remember *not* knowing about him! Then think about how you felt when you began to understand how much he loves you. At some point, most of you realized that you love him, too, and you decided to follow him. Each of us has our very own faith story—one that tells how our faith in Jesus has grown. Even if you don't know Jesus very well, you have a story about your faith. And since everyone's faith story is different, we'll use different ways to tell those special stories to others.**

Explain that kids can choose from four different stations where they can tell their faith stories. At the first station with the music playing, they can write their own song to share their faith story. At the station with the chairs and pillows, kids can take turns talking about their faith with others there. At the station with the art supplies, encourage kids to share their faith story through pictures and creativity. And at the fourth station, kids can write their story in a book. Show them how to make the book form by stacking a few blank white pages on top of a piece of construction paper, then folding all in half and stapling along the folded edge.

Encourage kids to sing, discuss, read, or show pictures of their stories with others at their stations. When kids are finished, ask:

• **Why are our faith stories so unique?**

• **Why is it important to share our stories with others?**

• **Who will you share your story with this week?**

Activity 2

WAITING...AND WAITING...AND WAITING

The Israelites waited a long time for the prophesied arrival of their King! Use this experience to help kids empathize with the Israelites and to understand why Jesus was a gift worth waiting for.

Before class, wrap individual treats kids would enjoy such as cookies or small toys so that each child can receive one. (If you have a large group of kids, wrap all the treats in one large gift.) Set the gifts in the front of your meeting area.

As kids arrive, raise their anticipation for the gifts you have for them. Say things such as "I'm so excited about the gifts I have for you today" and "What do you think is wrapped inside those gifts?"

When everyone has arrived, say: **I have a wonderful gift for each of you today, but you'll have to wait to open it. It'll be hard for me to wait, too, because I'm so excited to give them to all of you!**

Have kids form groups of four or five. Ask them to share with their groups about a time they had to wait a long time for something good to happen. For example, maybe someone had to wait all summer to take a special vacation to Disney World.

After groups share, say: **What if you had to wait for someone to come along and save your life? That's what happened to the Israelites in the Bible. The Israelites were God's chosen people. He helped them escape slavery in Egypt, and he made them kings in their own land. But many of the kings turned out to be evil rulers, and Israel became divided. And in spite of all God's blessings, many Israelites turned from him until finally they were led into captivity again. But God still loved them, and he promised to send them a Messiah—someone who would save them once and for all. The only thing is: He didn't say when. The Israelites were very excited about this special gift, but they had to wait a long time for it.**

Hold up a wrapped gift. Ask:

- **How does it feel to wait for our special gift right now?**
- **Do you think it's anything like the Israelites having to wait for their Messiah? Explain.**

Say: **The Israelites waited. And they waited. They waited for hundreds of years. Many generations came and went. They knew something good was coming. But they didn't know what the gift would look like or when they would receive the gift.** Ask:

- **Are you ready for your gift yet?**

Say: **Well, we'll have to wait a little bit longer. Right now, let's see what happened as a result of the Israelites waiting for so long.**

Have several volunteers take turns reading Luke 2:1-20 aloud. Then say: **He was finally here! The gift that was promised hundreds of years ago had finally arrived! The Messiah was born!** Ask:

• **How do you think the Israelites felt when their gift of Jesus finally arrived? Why?**

• **Imagine what it would be like if we were still waiting for the Messiah. How would you feel?**

Say: **You've waited a long time for your gifts. I'm sure you're pretty excited. Let's open them now!**

Have kids open their gifts. Before they enjoy their treats, say a prayer to thank God for sending the best gift of all—Jesus, the Messiah.

Activity 3

MY BOOK OF FAITH

Help kids remember what they learn and how they grow in their relationship with Jesus with this ongoing project.

Give each child a three-ring binder and explain that these will become their Books of Faith that they'll add to each week. In your classroom, always have these craft supplies available: different kinds of paper, child-friendly magazines, glue, glitter, scissors, crayons, paints, markers, and photocopies of the handout on the next page.

After each learning experience or lesson, encourage kids to add one page to their Books of Faith. Allow about 10 minutes after each lesson for kids to create their pages.

Prompt creativity by asking them to review what they've learned and how it affected their relationship with Jesus. Ask questions like:

- **What picture could you draw that shows your relationship with Jesus?**
- **Could you write a song about your relationship with Jesus?**
- **What would you like to remember about today's lesson? Write a poem or draw a picture about it.**
- **If you could write a letter to God about what you learned today, what would you say?**
- **What are five words you'd use to describe your relationship with Jesus?**

Continue adding to the Books of Faith as kids grow in your ministry. Every couple of months, take time for children to look through their books and reflect on what they've learned. You can also ask children to share with one another pages that are important to them.

When they leave your children's ministry to start a new journey in junior high, give them their Books of Faith to encourage them to keep growing closer to Jesus.

I WONDER...

I know...

I'm thankful for...

friend

trust

 faith

JOURNEY

grow

check it out

strong

AFRAID

sacrifice

 life

love

God's Word

gift

Activity 4

ONGOING SERVICE

Use this ongoing service project to help kids reach out to their communities.

Hang a huge sheet of newsprint on a wall (the bigger the better), and set paper and markers on the floor or a table nearby.

Have kids gather near the newsprint, and ask a volunteer to read aloud the fruits of the Spirit in Galatians 5:22-23.

Say: **When we have a relationship with Jesus, we show our faith in him by living lives filled with those fruits. Let's think of ways we can show the fruit of the Spirit in our lives. For example, one way you might show kindness is by sharing your lunch money with someone at school.**

Have kids form groups of four or five. Give each group a sheet of paper and markers. Encourage each group to come up with nine different ways to show the fruit of the Spirit in their lives. (They don't have to represent all nine different kinds of fruit listed in the passage.)

Then have groups share with everyone else the practical ways they can show the fruit in their lives. Write down everything they say somewhere on your newsprint.

Explain that each week, kids should choose one of the activities listed and do it during the week, showing others the fruit of God's Spirit in their lives. The following week, take time for kids to tell about what they did.

Encourage kids to continue thinking of ways to show the fruit in their lives in the weeks to come. As they think of new ways, have them write them on the newsprint.

Activity 5

TEACH IT THEIR WAY

Divide the kids into groups. Give each group strips of paper and pens. Have Group One come up with get-to-know-you questions. Group Two will think of hypothetical answers to get-to-know-you questions, but they won't know the questions that Group One has come up with yet. Encourage kids to think creatively—for example, questions shouldn't focus on names, ages, or where people are from.

When groups finish, put the questions in one bowl and the answers in another. Have one person from each group come to the bowls. The person from Group One will randomly pick a question and read it aloud. The person from Group Two will randomly pick an answer and read it aloud. The sillier the results, the better! Ask:

- **How much better do you know others after going through those questions? Why?**
- **Why is it important to get to know people personally?**

Give kids a photocopy of the "Get to Know You" handout. Have them find a different person to answer each question and write that person's name next to his or her answers. (You'll collect these later to get to know your students.)

When students have every question answered, ask:

- **Which way of getting to know others was better—our first try or our second? Why?**
- **If you could ask Jesus a get-to-know-you question, what would it be?**
- **What one thing will you do this week to get to know Jesus?**

Collect the handouts, and use them to learn more about your students.

Get to Know You

Directions: Ask people around you the following questions. Write down their answers and their names. Make sure you find a new person for each question!

What's your favorite thing to do at home?

What's your favorite thing to do at school?

If you were to tell a friend about Jesus, what would you say?

If you had $1,000, what would you do with it?

What is one thing you really want to learn about God?

Activity 6

YOU'RE INVITED!

Use this activity to encourage kids to reach out in their communities and invite others to church in creative ways. Ask:

- **If you had all the money in the world to spend on creative ways of inviting people to our church, how would you spend it?**

Have kids form groups of four or five, and have groups spread out around your meeting area. Explain that groups will create spectacular ways to invite people to their church. They'll pretend to have all the money and resources they need to make these invitations, which could be in the form of cards, TV commercials, billboards, or even skywriting! Encourage kids to use their imaginations as they create their invitations.

Give kids 10 minutes to work together. As they create, help groups think "outside the box." Remind them that they "have" all the money in the world.

When time is up, have groups present their ideas. They can act them out, show their artwork, or just tell about the idea.

When groups finish, say: **You all came up with some very creative ways to invite people to our church! God wants us to help others get to know him. One way we can do that is by inviting them to learn about him and grow closer to him at church. Let's come up with some more ideas to invite others to church. This time, let's make these ideas things we can do this week.**

Have each group come up with three ideas of ways to invite others to church. Some examples might include sending an invitation to a neighbor, talking to a friend about Jesus, or leaving a note for a family member.

Say: **We all know people who don't know Jesus. This week, let's invite those people to come to church to learn about him. Choose one of the creative ways we came up with, and try it out this week.**

To use more collaborative learning and differentiated instruction, work with your class to choose one of the spectacular ideas your kids came up with and pull it off together!

Activity 7

WHEREVER

Before your meeting time, prepare the following areas of your room:
- Place dress-up costumes, stage makeup, and acting props in one corner. Provide as many items as possible. Set a Bible near these supplies.
- Make a puzzle out of poster board so that each child will receive a piece of the puzzle. Set markers and puzzle pieces in another corner of your meeting area.
- Create a pillar of fire by shredding red, orange, and yellow tissue paper and gluing it to a black poster board backing. Tape the poster to a wall opposite the costumes and props, and set up a flashlight so it's pointed directly at the pillar of fire.
- Create a pillar of cloud by gluing cotton balls to another black poster board backing. Set this next to the costumes and props.

As kids arrive, keep the room as dark as possible except for the light of the flashlight on the pillar of fire. Gather kids near the fire, and say: **Today we'll prove that God is always with us. Let's take a story from the Bible and find evidence that God never leaves us. It all starts with the Israelites escaping from Egypt. They didn't know where they were going. But God showed them the way. How did he do that?** Motion toward the poster of fire. **This fire gives us a hint. Let's follow our pillar of fire to the first part of our story.**

Give the flashlight to one of your students, and take the pillar of fire off the wall. Have the person with the flashlight keep shining it on the pillar of fire as you lead the kids to the costumes and props.

When you arrive, say: **Let's find out how God led the Israelites as they escaped from Egypt.** Have the student with the flashlight help you find and read Exodus 13:21-22. Then ask:
- **What would you think if God guided you to your friend's house with clouds and fire?**
- **How does God show *you* that he's always with you?**

Have kids form groups of four or five, and explain that they'll use the props to create a skit about the Israelites being guided by fire and a cloud. Give groups five minutes to create their skits, then have them present the skits to the rest of the group. As groups present, use the flashlight as a spotlight to set the mood of the theater.

When everyone is finished, say: **God was with the Israelites when they left Egypt. They needed guidance, and he helped them. We need guidance in our lives, too—and God is always with us.**

Turn on the lights and pick up the pillar of cloud you created. Use the cloud to lead kids to the puzzle pieces and markers. Give each student a puzzle piece, and explain that they should write or draw about a time they knew God was with them.

Give kids a few minutes to write and draw, then have kids work with each other to put the puzzle together. As they work, ask:

- **How did you know God was with you in the situation you wrote or drew about?**
- **How can you thank God for being with you in that situation?**

When the puzzle is finished, have kids look at all the ways God has guided others. Ask:

- **What do you notice about our puzzle?**

Say: **God loves us and knows what's best for us. He's with us all the time, and he guides us through every situation. Let's play a game to help us remember how God guided the Israelites.**

Choose one person to be the Pillar. Create a "sandwich" of the pillar of fire poster and the pillar of cloud poster by loosely connecting the two with tape at the top. Place it over the Pillar volunteer's shoulders like a sandwich advertising board.

Have everyone stand behind the Pillar at one end of your meeting area—that's Egypt. Explain that the goal is to try to reach the Promised Land on the other side of the room. But they can only travel during the day when the pillar of cloud faces them. If the Pillar turns around and they see the fire, it's nighttime and they must lie down and sleep. If the Pillar sees anyone traveling at night, the Pillar sends that person back to Egypt to try again. Everyone must stay behind the Pillar as they travel, because the Pillar is their guide.

Prompt the Pillar to alternately face the crowd and then quickly turn around to make the game more challenging. Play the game several times so different people can have a turn as the Pillar.

Then gather students in a circle, and ask:

- **What was it like to trust pillars of fire and cloud to get you to your goal?**
- **How does God show us that he's with us and that he'll guide us?**

Say: **Just as he led the Israelites and just as you showed in your puzzle, God is always with us. He guides us and helps us in our lives!**

Activity 8

WAY TO PRAY

Use this activity to make prayer personal for each child.

Set up the following prayer stations in separate corners of the room.

Station 1: Write these prayer starters on a few sheets of paper, and tape them to the walls around the station:

- I want to thank God for…
- I want to tell God…
- I need God…
- I need prayer for…

Station 2: Set out decorative paper and some nice pens.

Station 3: Set out art supplies, including paints and paintbrushes, sketch pads and pencils, and clay.

Station 4: Have reflective Christian music playing on a CD player.

Say: **Sometimes we get used to praying in the same ways over and over again. But we can be creative in the way we pray. God wants to hear us pray from our hearts.**

Explain that kids can choose a prayer station where they will find a unique way to pray to God. For example, at Station 1, kids will find four prayer starters. They can go to each of those prayer starters with a friend or by themselves, finishing the sentences aloud with others or silently.

At Station 2, kids can write a letter to God, telling him what's on their hearts. Encourage them to write as they would write to a friend.

At Station 3, kids can use the various art supplies to create an artistic prayer to God. They can express their feelings through painting, draw a picture of what they want to pray for, or sculpt something they love about God.

Finally, at Station 4, students will create motions to go along with a praise song.

Give kids as much time as they need to talk to God. Allow them to switch stations as often as they like. When the prayer time is over, ask:

- **What was special about your prayer time?**
- **What is one new way you'll talk to God from your heart this week?**

Activity 9

JESUS' LAST DAYS

Use this activity to help kids understand how strong God's love is for them.

Have kids form groups of four, and give each group a Bible and a "Neither...Nor" handout.

Say: **God loves us more than we can imagine. He loves us so much that he sent his only Son to die in our place so we can be with him forever. That kind of love can't be taken away or broken. Let's explore that more.**

Give groups five minutes to work through their handouts. Then have the kids in each group number themselves from one to four. Have all the ones form a group, the twos form another group, the threes another, and the fours a final group.

Have kids tell their new groups one of the "neither...nor" statements they came up with. Give them a couple minutes to share. Then have them tell one way they'll show God their love in return this week.

Neither...Nor

1 God's love never ends. Nothing can separate you from his love. Nothing you do. Nothing you say. Nothing! Ever! Check it out in **Romans 8:38-39**. Read the passage with your group, switching readers every time you get to a comma.

3 Answer these questions in your group:
- What's the greatest thing God has done to show his love for *you*?
- How does it feel to know that nothing can separate us from God's love?

2 Now come up with your own "neither...nor" statements. We started it for you here:
Nothing can separate us from God's love. Neither bullies nor friends. Neither...

_____
_____
_____
_____
_____
_____
_____
_____
_____
_____
_____
_____

4 Take turns praying in your group. Tell God how you feel about his love. Then let him know what you'll do to show your love in return.

Activity 10

OUT-REEEEEEACH

Use this game to help kids understand how working together helps us reach out to others.

Pour individually wrapped candies into enough bowls so that teams of five kids will each have one. Set the bowls in a parallel line 30 feet from a wall.

Have kids form teams and line up along the wall. Tell kids that each team is welcome to a bowl of candy, but teammates must work together to reach the bowl. Here are the rules: One person must continually touch the wall, and the entire team must remain connected through the experience. When they reach the bowl, they must stay connected as they bring it back to the wall. Encourage them to use their imaginations in order to overcome the challenge—for example, they may take off shoelaces or necklaces and stretch these between each other as they form a chain toward the candy.

Signal teams to start, and give them several minutes to complete the task. If reaching the bowl was too easy, increase the distance or decrease the group size.

When groups are finished, allow them to enjoy their candy as they discuss the following questions. Ask:

• **What was easy or hard about reaching the candy?**

• **Why was it important to work together in this activity?**

• **How can we work together to reach others for God?**

Say: **God wants the church to work together to help others grow closer to Jesus. The Bible tells us to motivate each other to love and good works. Let's read that now.**

Have a volunteer read Hebrews 10:24-25, and then ask:

• **Why do we need to work together with other Christians?**

• **How will you motivate Christian friends or family members this week to show love to others and do good works?**

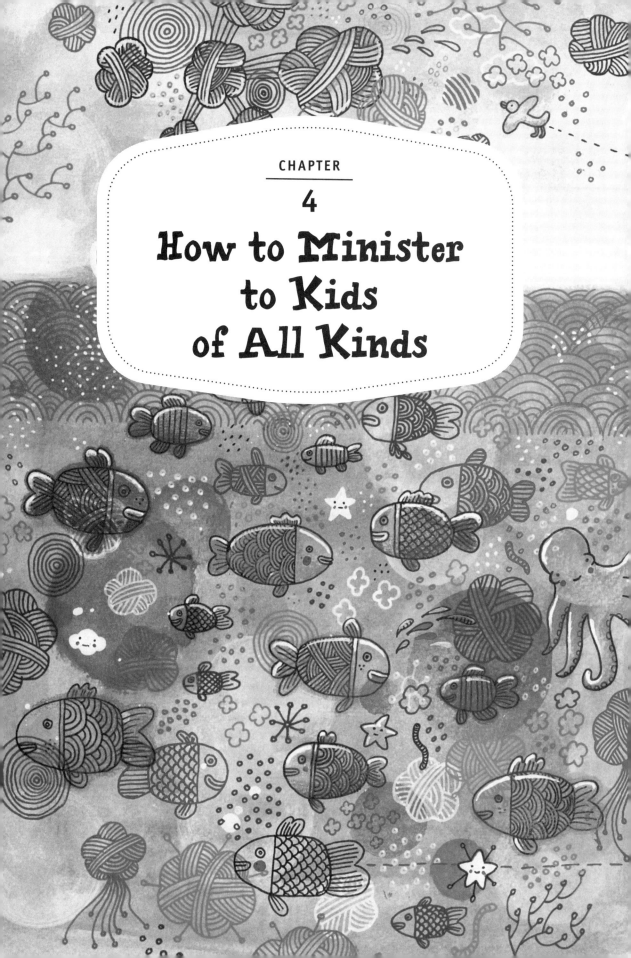

CHAPTER

4

How to Minister to Kids of All Kinds

TOMORROW'S KIDS

BY PAT VERBAL

"Serving and loving one child may even impact the future of the nation and shape generations yet unborn." (Dr. H.B. London Jr., *For Kids' Sake*)

In the spring of 2006, a new TV program aired called *Little People, Big World*. In this upbeat series, viewers met Amy and Matt Roloff and their four children. Three of their children have a normal growth pattern while one, Zach, is a little person. He's a twin, and at age 15, he finds that height increasingly separates him from his brother, Jeremy. Matt says that when you're only 4 feet tall, it's easy to feel like the world wasn't made for you.

Have you considered that some children in your church may feel like they're living in a world that wasn't made for them? They've heard about God's love and plan for their lives, but they feel excluded, invisible, and devalued. In this chapter, you'll meet children with unique challenges who may get left behind in the process of "doing" church. You'll also discover ways we can fulfill the great commission to help 21st-century children make Zach's choices—to accept themselves as God made them and to embrace their faith.

SPECIAL KIDS IN THE NEIGHBORHOOD

Madison's family moved to the city near a school for children with cerebral palsy. She loved her new house, but missed her old church where the first-graders always made her feel accepted. They ran around her wheelchair playing games and helped her with crafts. At her new church, Madison sat by the window hoping her classmates would just talk to her. Madison's parents encouraged her to be patient. But then a flier for vacation Bible school came home with this footnote: "We can only register as many children with special needs as we have volunteers for." At first her parents were hurt to think their daughter might miss something she looked forward to every summer. Then they were angry with what they saw as unethical—and possibly illegal—discrimination.

Churches in the 21st century must understand that children with special needs are in every neighborhood in America. We can no longer send these families to the church across town while we do nothing to accommodate them. According to the Centers for Disease Control and Prevention, 17 percent of U.S. children are afflicted with a disability. Autism is the fastest growing disability, but others are escalating as well. There is a broad spectrum of developmental disabilities that may affect a child's speech, physical growth, psychological growth, self-care, learning, and general health.

Rate of Children With Disabilities	(per 1,000)
Autism	3.4
Mental Retardation	9.7
Cerebral Palsy	3.8
Hearing/Vision	1.1
Down Syndrome	1.2
Vision Impairment	0.9

(Statistics from the Centers for Disease Control and Prevention)

Jacob bore his burden of asthma, dyslexia, and ADHD on skinny shoulders. The four medications he took suppressed his appetite, and when he forgot them, he got violent. He hit teachers, hurled books, and cursed. To his single mom's shock, his school expelled Jacob three times and placed him in alternative school. Yet, as she visited churches, she thrust him into a classroom without a word about his condition to the teachers. This is a common occurrence, and teachers are at a loss when problems arise.

WHAT CAN WE DO?

1. Break down walls. In Dr. Wess Stafford's book, *Too Small to Ignore,* he talks about the importance of caring relationships. "When children are part of a close-knit group, they feel safe and know they are not abandoned. They enjoy life in the shadows of taller people who genuinely care about what happens to them. The poor, the weak, the small, and the young receive the benefit of common concern."

One day as a Christian mentor prayed with Jacob, he asked that God would give Jacob peace. When he finished praying, Jacob asked, "What's peace?" His friend explained that when we have God's peace, we're calm on the inside when everything isn't calm on the outside. Jacob smiled and said, "Will you pray that prayer again, because I didn't understand it the first time."

2. Accept children. See children for who they are without labels or judgment. "For we are God's masterpiece. He has created us anew in Christ Jesus, so we can do the good things he planned for us long ago" (Ephesians 2:10). It was when Jacob felt loved by his mentor that the walls came down.

3. Connect with parents. Maintain a healthy dialogue with parents, make home visits, and design unique Christian educational goals for every child.

4. Educate others. Provide church-wide awareness and trained teachers who not only welcome children with special needs but also help them know and serve Jesus Christ.

One way Arlyn Kantz of Precision Songs does this is by hosting a VBS for children with autism at her church. "Our staff ratio is one adult to every two students, and parents fill out a detailed registration form so we can tailor our teaching strategies to the needs of each child," says Kantz. "We use a music curriculum called Sing to Know What I Believe that puts basic theological concepts to music and helps children understand the gospel." (www.precisionsongs.com)

WHO WILL HELP US?

- Special education teachers in neighborhood schools are a wealth of information and encouragement. Invite them to lead training seminars.

- Respite care leaders in local churches need volunteers and can provide on-the-job training. Respite care is a program designed to give parents a night out while their children are cared for at church.

- Joni and Friends ministry provides tools to start special needs ministries, support groups, and family retreats. (www.joniandfriends.org)

- Special Education Today (SET) is a magazine for church leaders that addresses special education needs from a Christian perspective. (www.lifeway.com)

ABUSED CHILDREN

From the outside, Abby's fourth-grade world looked pretty good. Although her parents divorced the year before, Abby was popular, bright, athletic, and shopped at Abercrombie & Fitch. Her birthday party included a spa day with a dozen friends and a night at Dave and Buster's restaurant.

Abby especially enjoyed acting in the plays at church, until one day when the pressure seemed too much. She missed a line at dress rehearsal, ran from the stage in tears, and locked herself in the restroom. As the sobs grew louder and Abby began beating her head against the wall, her children's pastor softly prayed through the door.

When Abby calmed down, she shared her fear of her mother's new boyfriend. His playful attentions had turned into sexual advances with threats of what he would do if she told anyone. Abby also felt guilty because at first she liked the attention, but now she hated this man and wanted him out of her life. Fortunately, Abby told a trusted adult, who knew how to help her and her mom through the crisis.

Darren's story of abuse is every church's nightmare. A children's choir volunteer, who had passed a background check, molested Darren over the course of a year. The molestation took place at a large, well-known church after choir rehearsals. In the week that followed, several boys confessed to also being abused by the predator.

It is estimated that child sexual abuse is reported up to 80,000 times a year. When parents are absent, the risk increases. If the abuse is kept secret, children may become depressed, withdrawn, untrusting, and experience sleep or eating disorders.

WHAT CAN WE DO?

Confront signs of abuse and inappropriate behavior. Rather than viewing these children's experiences as isolated events, leaders need to consider that many other children may be experiencing similar struggles. You are a mandatory reporter of child abuse to Child Protection Services; follow your ministry's reporting procedures. Respect a child's privacy and keep confidences. We can be the arms of Jesus to hurting children.

WHO WILL HELP US?

- The children's council at your church must create effective policies for volunteer screening, conduct, and reporting.

- ACTION is a child safety organization that operates the National Child Welfare Resource Center for Child Protective Services. They offer consulting, training, and technical support. (www.actionchildprotection.org)

- Group's Church Volunteer Central offers volunteer background checks, including a sexual offender database search. (www.group.com/cvc)

- Christian counselors will work with churches to provide therapy options and financial assistance to families in need.

- Child protection specialists at Yello Dyno offer non-fearful, non-explicit, and uplifting safety education for children ages 4 to 12. (www.yellodyno.com)

CHILDREN'S OBESITY

For several decades we've heard about eating disorders such as anorexia and bulimia. But as today's kids would say, "That's so 30 seconds ago!" Move over skinny—it's time for super size!

Brian is a leader in the most common health problem facing U.S. children today. At 4' 9" and 116 pounds, Brian is obese, which is defined as 20 percent above average for the child's height. He eats two school lunches and towers over the children in his class. After school, talks with his mom sound like this:

Mom: *I washed an apple for your snack, honey. Later, let's ride our bikes to the park, OK?*

Brian: *I'm starving! When's dinner? Where are the chips? Can we order pizza? My favorite show is on TV, OK?*

It's a Happy Meal world for kids like Brian, who are enticed by every new fast-food creation, but super sizing comes with a price. The U.S. Surgeon General says, "We are seeing Generation Y growing into Generation XL."

Generation "XL" kids:
- make up 13 percent of today's children
- are expected to develop Type 2 diabetes
- are at risk for heart disease, stroke, asthma, and arthritis
- usually have family issues with weight control
- often make poor lifestyle choices
- are often targets of school bullies' cruel jokes

A growing number of parents fight a constant battle to get their children to eat right and stay active. Some throw up their hands and quit. But they aren't giving up in the fight against bullies, who make life miserable for their kids. "My son hates recess!" says one mom. "And he doesn't finish his assignments so he can work in the library during lunch. Kids make 'oinking' sounds, tell 'fat' jokes, and even throw things at him. Some days he's afraid to use the restroom because he thinks bullies will beat him up."

According to researcher George Barna, "Forty-five percent of elementary schools reported one or more incidents of violent crime; the figure balloons to 74 percent, three-quarters, of all middle schools...More than 1 million adolescents missed at least one day of school this past year due to fear of physical violence."

WHAT CAN WE DO?

1. Teach children that God loves them and that he looks at the heart, not the outward appearance. (1 Samuel 16:7)

2. Model a healthy lifestyle and serve nutritional snacks at church.

3. Assure children that God is with them to protect them and help them stand up for what is right. (Psalm 23:4; Ephesians 6:13)

4. Help children, parents, and teachers learn about bullying. The church must have a zero tolerance policy.

5. Call children to respond with empathy to one another and be respectful. (2 Timothy 2:24)

6. Sponsor workshops on health and fitness, sports programs, and active family game nights.

WHO WILL HELP US?

- National bestsellers on childhood obesity such as *SuperSized Kids* by Larimore and Flynt are good resources for parenting classes.

- Public schools will share copies of their policy on handling bullies.

- The Parent Advocacy Coalition for Educational Rights (PACER) created a kid-friendly Web site especially for children who are being targeted by bullying. (www.pacerkidsagainstbullying.org)

- Upward Basketball is an evangelistic ministry leader in sports programs that make children feel like winners. They provide programs in basketball, soccer, flag football, and cheerleading. (www.upward.org)

CHILDREN IN TRANSITION

Alina represents an overwhelming number of children who are forced to make drastic changes in their lives. She is one of the 5,000 orphans adopted from Russia by American families each year. On her first Sunday at church, she clung to her new mom, unable to communicate with the other children. Her thin frame and sullen eyes hinted at her sad memories of nine years in an orphanage. Alina faced many challenges in her new homeland, but she was one of the lucky ones. The family who adopted her loved the Lord and had prayed for her for four years.

Daniel's move was more of a surprise. After his father died in a car accident and his mother started using drugs, he moved in with his grandparents. Daniel felt embarrassed at first, but he knew his grandparents loved him. They never missed a parent-teacher conference or school program. Eventually, his grandparents adopted him, and he was glad to call them Mom and Dad.

Before the hurricane destroyed her home in New Orleans, Chantel went to church every Sunday. Her mom even sang in the choir. Following the tragedy, Chantel moved four times, changed schools twice, and misses her extended family, which is now spread across three states. Her family spends holidays and birthdays in their tiny apartment, because her mom is still out of work. But the hardest thing for Chantel to understand is why they never go to church anymore.

WHAT CAN WE DO?

Give hope and support to adoptive parents, grandparents, and displaced families. Alina's church raised money for her trip from Russia and hosted a welcome party where she was showered with gifts. And although Chantel's mom is discouraged, a member of a nearby church calls her regularly just to chat.

Daniel's grandparents are in a Life Group that prays for them and drives him to baseball practices. Grandparents like Daniel's are called "rewinders" and face issues that include grandparent rights, guardianship, adoption, power of attorney, medical consent, and legal custody. Parenting specialist Dr. Mary Manz Simons encourages rewinders to participate in children's activities. "Children of rewinders want to be viewed as 'real' families," says Simons. "Seeing Grandpa work alongside other parents at a school picnic validates the family...The increasing number of rewinders presents an emerging social issue that brings together two vulnerable populations: the young and the old. We should remember these families in our prayers and offer support as we are able."

 Teach children to value others, feel their pain, and prayerfully consider how Jesus would respond. This generation may be the most open-minded ever. The world is not black and white to them. Many American kids are to be commended for doing their best to build close relationships with kids of many different races and lifestyles. While prejudice still exists, it has no place in the church.

WHO WILL HELP US?

- Church-wide programs such as *Friendship First* help children and adults build friendships with one another and with God. (www.friendshipfirst.com)

- The Rorheim Institute is addressing disturbing family trends unmet in churches. They offer regional Shepherding Parents Seminars to train and equip the next generation of parents and leaders. (www.awana.org)

- In the Children's Defense Fund's effort to support the one in 12 children living with grandparents and other relatives, they created a Kinship Care Kit. The kit is designed to help churches provide support and resources. (http://www.childrensdefense .org/site/PageServer?pagename=homepage)

- Disaster-relief organizations, such as The Salvation Army and the American Red Cross, partner with churches in times of natural disasters.

STANDING ON GOD'S WORD

As we minister to children with such vast needs, the thing that remains constant and stable is the Bible. Cling to it, and don't water it down. It was the psalmist David who first asked, "The foundations of law and order have collapsed. What can the righteous do?" (Psalm 11:3). Generations later, Timothy boldly responded, "But God's truth stands firm like a foundation stone with this inscription: 'The Lord knows those who are his' " (2 Timothy 2:19).

Watching this generation reminds me of our family's vacations to Tampa Bay's Busch Gardens. As we waited in line to ride their mammoth roller coaster, children all around us squealed in fear—but they kept moving forward. Some kids only got on because a trusted adult crawled in beside them. The wild ride never disappointed them with its jerky climbs and plunging falls. At the exit gate, their faces were flushed and their knees wobbled, but they patted one another on the back for braving the danger.

Tomorrow's kids are on a fast ride through childhood, with problems and promises we could never have envisioned for them. With God's love, we can strap ourselves into the seat next to them, grasp their hands, and help them hold on to their faith.

RESOURCES FOR FURTHER STUDY

American Academy of Child & Adolescent Psychiatry (www.aacap.org/publications/factsfam/sexabuse.htm)

Barna, George, *Transforming Children into Spiritual Champions*. Ventura, CA: Regal Books, 2003.

London, H. B. Jr. and Wiseman, Neil B., *For Kids' Sake: Winning the Tug-of-War for Future Generations*. Ventura, CA: Regal Books, 2004.

Simon, Mary Manz, *Trend-Savvy Parenting: An Insider's Guide to Changes That Shape Your Child's World*. Wheaton, IL: Tyndale House Publishers, 2006.

Stafford, Wess, T*oo Small to Ignore: Why Children Are the Next Big Thing*. Colorado Springs, CO: Waterbrook Press, 2005.

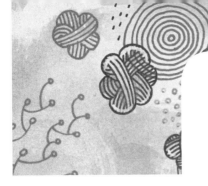

Try This

BY JANNA KINNER

BE SILENT NAME GAME

Before the lesson, make one copy of the American Sign Language Alphabet handout for each child.

Form groups of two or three. Instruct the children to take turns telling their group members how to spell their name. The catch is, they can't talk or write it down! Give each of the children a few moments to communicate the spelling of their name to their group.

Then ask:

- **What did it feel like to not be able to talk or write?**
- **What are some ways you communicated to your group members without talking or writing?**
- **What are some ways people communicate to others when they can't hear?**

Give each pair a Bible and have them read Genesis 11:1-9 together.

Say: **We didn't always speak different languages. As you've discovered from your reading, long ago, everyone in the world spoke the same language! But the people were prideful and disobedient, and they decided to build a huge tower as a monument to themselves. God didn't think that was a good idea, so he scattered them all over the earth speaking languages they didn't all understand. To this day, we don't always understand each other—God made everyone different, but we still try to communicate. Some people aren't able to speak or hear well. People who are deaf use sign language to help them communicate to people around them. Let's learn the sign language alphabet so we can communicate with people who can't hear.**

Give each child an American Sign Language Alphabet handout. Go through the letters as a class, then give each group several minutes to practice spelling their names to each other. (If you know someone who's hearing impaired, you might ask that person to help teach the alphabet to your class.) Ask:

- **Why is it important to learn to speak to others, even if we don't speak the same language they do?**
- **What can you do to make people who are deaf or speak another language feel comfortable in our church?**

Say: **God wants us to work together to tell others about Jesus, even if we don't speak the same language. Just as we learned from the Bible story today, people work together better when they know how to communicate.**

American Sign Language

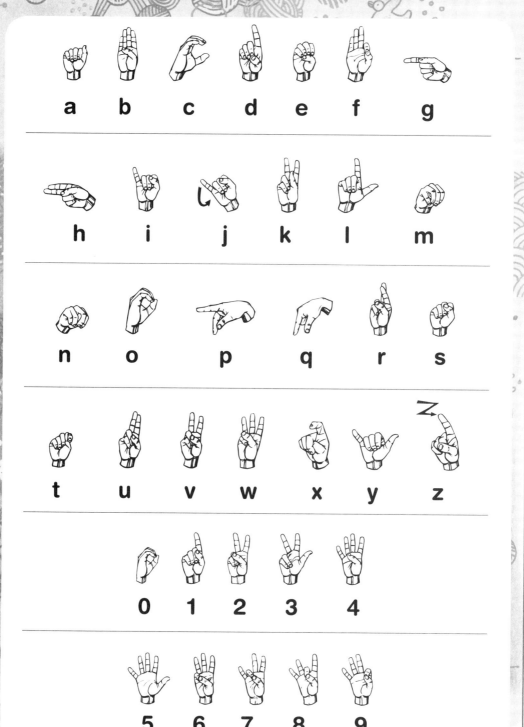

Activity 2

CAN'T USE IT!

Use this activity to help kids understand the difficulties others face who have physical disabilities. (If you have a child in your class who faces this type of challenge, that child will have the chance to shine on a level playing field where he or she is already adept.)

Form four groups. Each child will have a bandanna tied around a body part according to the following groups. Explain that you'll all pretend to have specific disabilities as you try to accomplish a task together. Say the following statement to the respective groups:

- Group 1: **You're not able to use your arms.** Loosely tie their wrists together.

- Group 2: **You've lost the use of your right leg.** Tie the bandanna around one leg.

- Group 3: **You can't use either of your legs.** Tie the bandanna around both legs (or tie the ankles together loosely).

- Group 4: **You can't see.** Blindfold each child.

Say: **Let's spread God's Word! Your team needs to get your stack of five Bibles from one side of the room to the other. However, you're not allowed to use the body part that your bandanna is tied onto, and you must move the Bibles in a respectful manner. For example, if you have a bandanna on your wrists, you can't use your arms to pick up the Bibles, but you can't kick the Bible, either, because that would be disrespectful. If you have a bandanna around your legs, you can't walk.**

Give the children several minutes to accomplish moving the Bibles. Since each group will be unique in how they do this relay, encourage teamwork and creativity—winning is not the objective.

After everyone finishes the relay, have the children sit in their groups. Ask each group to report what their disability was and what they did to overcome it. For example, the group that was blind might have felt along the walls to get to the other side. The group without use of their legs might scoot across the floor using their arms with a Bible on their back.

- **What was the hardest part about this relay? the easiest part?**
- **How do people who are disabled (blind, deaf, or paralyzed) accomplish things?**
- **How was this relay like spreading God's Word to our friends and neighbors, no matter how hard that might be?**

- **How can people who are disabled spread God's Word?**

Hand out a Bible to each group and allow time for the children to look up and read 1 Corinthians 12:18-21. Ask:

- **Why did God make all of us different?**
- **If Jesus couldn't walk, do you think he'd still tell others about God? Why or why not?**
- **Close your eyes. If this is what you saw every day, could you still tell others about Jesus? How?**

Say: **Just like you were able to overcome your disability in this game, people who are disabled do amazing things every day. Even though God made us all different, he gave each of us things that we are especially good at. He wants us to all work together for his glory, no matter how hard we think that might be.**

Activity 3

BLIND ART

Supplies: chalk, chalkboard or sidewalk to draw on, one piece of paper per pair, one pencil per pair, one blindfold per pair

Have children pair up and blindfold one in each pair. Have the other child use a pencil to secretly draw on a piece of paper one triangle, one square, and one circle. The child can decide how big to make those shapes and where to position them on the paper. Now give the blindfolded child a piece of chalk and a drawing space on a chalkboard or on the sidewalk. Allow time for the blindfolded child to attempt to draw exactly what is drawn on his or her partner's paper, based on verbal instructions from the partner. Then he or she can remove the blindfold to see how close the drawing came.

If time allows, switch partners so the other child can be blindfolded. Ask:

- **What was it like to do this drawing while you were blindfolded?**
- **When your partner was describing what his or her drawing looked like, what clues were helpful? What clues would have been helpful?**
- **How might this be like helping a person who is blind?**

Read John 9:1-3 to the class.

Say: **We're all different, aren't we? But no matter what situation we're in, God can use that situation for his glory. Just as he did with the blind man in the Bible, God lets his power show through people who need him. And the more we understand challenges such as blindness, the more we can help, too.**

Activity 4

PUPPIES, KITTENS, AND KIDDOS

Let kids discover the parallel between animals who need loving homes and people who need loving homes, too.

Take your class on a field trip to the Humane Society. Give each of the children a small notebook or a piece of paper and a pencil to take with them. Allow time for the children to look at all the animals there. Ask a staff member or volunteer to talk to the children about how they find the animals and how the animals can be adopted. If time allows, encourage each child to draw a picture of their favorite animal before you leave. For extra impact, use a Polaroid camera to take a picture of the child standing next to the animal.

Back in the classroom, encourage the children to write a story about how their animal came to be at the Humane Society. Details might include where it was born, who it lived with, and how it was lost or abandoned.

Allow time for each of the children to report on their animal and show the picture they drew.

Then ask:

- **What did you like about our trip to the Humane Society? What did you not like?**
- **When you were listening to everyone's stories about the animals there, what things were the same? What things were different?**

Say: **Every animal at the Humane Society is different. They each had different families that they lived with, and they will each go to live with different families. That's like our class, too. Everyone here has a family unlike any other. Your family is unique—it might not look like the family next door. In fact, your family might not look the same this year as it did last year. Jesus loves all of the animals at the Humane Society, but he loves you even more. Isn't it good to know that no matter how our families might change, Jesus is the same?**

Activity 5

MIXTURE MANIA

Help kids discover how their different qualities and unique backgrounds combine with others' to make God's kingdom a real treat!

Before class, place each of the following trail mix ingredients in a separate baggie (you'll want enough baggies so that each child will have one): dry oat, corn, or rice cold cereal; chocolate-coated morsels; raisins; chocolate chips; pretzels; popcorn; and so on).

Place a large mixing bowl in the center of the room and have the children form a circle around it. Say: **This bowl has a lot of potential. It could really be something amazing, but right now it's kind of boring, isn't it? Let's liven things up.**

Give each child a baggie of trail mix ingredients. Have the children take turns saying something about themselves that makes them unique; something that is different from anyone else in the class. As kids mention their special qualities, have them pour the contents of their baggies into the bowl. After each child has added ingredients to the bowl, say: **Wow—the bowl already looks more interesting, doesn't it? Look at all the different types of yummy food inside! But I think we can do even better.**

Have a child stir the ingredients together and refill kids' baggies with a spoonful of new trail mix. Meanwhile, ask another volunteer to read Psalm 139:14. As kids munch on their treats, say: **Each ingredient in our trail mix was processed in a special way. Raisins were harvested as grapes and then dried into something totally different. Cereals are grains from the field that have been baked and formed into shapes. Chocolate candies come from a mixture of lots of things, including cocoa and sugar. Everything you're eating right now has a different and unique background!** Ask:

- **How are people in this class like the ingredients of our trail mix?**
- **Why is it good that God made everyone unique, with different backgrounds and families?**
- **How can we show that we appreciate differences in others?**

Pray together, thanking God for making everyone unique and special.

Activity 6

MISSION: FINDING JESUS' HEALINGS

In this lesson, kids will discover how important it was to Jesus to minister to *all* people—including those who were ill or physically challenged.

Before the lesson, photocopy the Bible Exploration chart on the next page so that each child will have one.

Form the children into groups. Say: **Jesus loves everyone, no matter what their situation is. When he met people in the Bible who needed him, he always took the time to help. Let's find examples of some of his healings in the Bible.**

Hand out Bible Exploration charts, pencils, and a Bible to each group. Assign each group one passage to look up. Allow time for each group to look up its Bible passage and fill in the first two columns: *Challenge or Sickness* and *What Jesus Did to Help*. Instruct groups to keep the last column blank until the end of the activity.

When each group has completed the row corresponding to its passage, have the kids form new groups composed of one person from each previous group. In other words, there should be at least one representative in each new group for the four passages on the chart. Have each new group member share the passage he or she worked on so that the others can complete their charts.

When everyone has finished, ask:

• **Why do you think Jesus cares so much about people who are sick or hurting?**
• **When you're sick or hurting, how can you ask Jesus to help you?**

Now give the groups time to fill in the last column: *What We Can Do to Help*. Encourage each group to pick one of the activities in this column to do this week. For example, they might choose to make a card for someone in the hospital, share video games with someone who can't play outside, etc. Have them write down their plan. Post the plans on the wall—next week, have the class discuss how the plans were carried out.

Bible Passage	Challenge or Sickness	What Jesus Did to Help	What We Can Do to Help
John 9:1-25			
Mark 7:31-37			
Mark 2:1-12			
Mark 1:40-45			

Activity 7

DIVERSITY POSTER

First John 4:7 encourages us to continue to love one another, for love comes from God. Remind kids that this means more than loving our families or our best friends—it means loving *everyone*, even (or especially!) those we feel are "different" from us. Use this activity to help kids identify who this verse is talking about. You'll need the following supplies: large poster board, glue sticks, scissors, magazines, newspapers, and a large permanent marker.

Say: **Love comes from God, and God wants us to love everyone. Let's make something that'll show who that "everyone" is. We'll take several minutes to look through these magazines and newspapers. Cut out any pictures or articles about people who you think are different from you—look for people of different races or nationalities, different abilities or challenges, different religions, and different ages. All of these things represent diversity, so when you find them, glue them to our poster.**

Pass out the magazines and newspapers, and allow several minutes for the children to look for pictures representing diversity. After they've cut out the pictures or articles, help kids glue them to the poster in a collage.

When the poster board is full, put away the magazines and other supplies. Ask:

- **How does our poster show diversity? In what ways are these people the same?**
- **Think of people you know who seem very different from you. What makes them seem different? How might they think you're different from them?**
- **If you met Jesus walking along the street, would he seem different from you? Explain.**

Say: **God made us all unique. We can see by looking at this poster that people have different ages and nationalities and religions. But God loves all of us the same. He calls us his children.**

In the middle of the poster, over the pictures, write "1 John 4:7." Read that verse aloud, and remind the children that God loves everyone, no matter what we look like or how diverse we are.

Activity 8

DON'T LEAVE ME OUT!

The Bible tells us how people with certain ailments were excluded from the rest of society—often cruelly. Leviticus 13:45-46 talks specifically about the rules lepers had to follow. Sometimes, even unknowingly, kids exclude others from their cliques or groups, following unspoken "rules" of acceptable appearance, abilities, or personalities. What does it feel like to be on the outside of such a clique? Let kids discover for themselves.

Form circles of six or seven each. Tell kids to "scrunch" together, putting their arms around each other to make tight circles facing inward. Say: **You all look like a tight group of friends! But what happens when there's an outcast? I'll call out a description, and the person who matches my description must step out of the circle and then try to push his or her way into the middle of the circle. The rest of the circle should close up and not let that person in.**

Call out different descriptions, such as the person:
- wearing the most red/other color
- with the longest hair
- who's the tallest/shortest
- who's the oldest/youngest

Create your own descriptions to give as many children as possible the experience of being left out of the circle. After a bit, gather kids together and ask:
- **How did it feel to be left out of the circle?**
- **What did it feel like to leave people out of your circle?**
- **If Jesus tried to get into your circle, what would you have done? Why?**
- **Tell a partner what you can do the next time someone's left out of your group of friends.**

Say: **In our game today, we experienced how hurtful it can be to be left out. We can all learn to include others around us by inviting them to play with us and by talking to them about what's going on in their life. Let's practice by asking someone you don't know very well about their school or their family.**

Allow several minutes for the kids to get to know one another.

Activity 9

WORRIES, WORRIES

Before this lesson, tape the lid onto a shoe box. Cut a strip in the top so an envelope can pass through it. Label the box "Dear God..."

Read Philippians 4:6-7 aloud. Say: **Isn't it a good feeling to know that no matter what we're going through, whether it's at home, at school, or even here at church, we can tell God about it and he'll give us peace. That doesn't always mean the problem goes away, but he helps you deal with it in a way that makes you feel better. Let's give our worries to God right now, telling him what we need and thanking him for what he's done.**

Give each child a piece of paper, a pencil, and one envelope. Ask the children to spread out around the room so they each have personal space. Say: **Take a few minutes to write down or draw a picture of something you're worried about. On the other side of your paper, write or draw something you'd like to thank God for. No one else will read your paper.**

Allow several peaceful minutes for them to do so. Meanwhile, prepare a CD player with a mellow worship CD.

Say: **Let's take time right now to pray about your worries. When I turn on the music, pray silently for a few minutes about the worry you wrote on your paper. Then seal your paper in your envelope and deposit it in this box to remind you that you've given your worry to God. No one will read your worry paper; this is between you and God.**

Turn on some soft music and allow the kids time to pray and put their envelopes in the box. When everyone has completed this, lead the children in this prayer: **Dear God, thank you for taking our worries. Help us to feel your peace. Amen.**

Remind the children that they can pray about their worries any time. Also tell them that they can talk to you or another adult about their worries after class.

Activity 10

WHY DO BAD THINGS HAPPEN?

Use this activity to help kids understand that God is always with us.

Before the lesson, attach a poster board to the wall by taping only along the poster's top edge. Place one magnet (large enough for all kids to see) in the top corner of the poster board, and place the other magnet in the same position on the back of the poster board so they hold each other in place by magnetic energy. Practice sliding one of the magnets along the poster board—the other magnet should follow on the reverse side.

Gather the children in front of the poster. Ask:

- **What are some bad things that happen sometimes? It could be something that happened or could happen to you, or it could be something bad that's happened to someone else, or it could be something that you worry about.** As kids mention things, write them with marker in various spots on the poster board.

When the poster board is full, say: **There are a lot of bad things that can happen to us in our lives.** Reach underneath the poster and read aloud some of the things you've written on the poster board. As you mention each situation, move the magnet on the back of the poster so that the front magnet travels to the written words. Mention six or seven of the bad things or worries written on the poster. Ask:

- **How do you feel when bad things happen? Why?**
- **Where is God when bad things happen?**

Say: **When bad things happen, we might feel sad or lonely. But during everything that we go through in our lives, we can know that we're not alone.** Indicate the magnet on the front of the poster. **Even when this magnet was moving around all the bad things on the front of this poster, the other magnet was with it all the time.** Turn the poster board over to reveal the second magnet.

Ask a volunteer to read aloud Isaiah 41:10. Ask:

- **How was our activity like or unlike God's promise to be with us during hard times?**
- **What can we do when we feel lonely or worried?**

Lead the children in a prayer thanking God for being with us all the time.

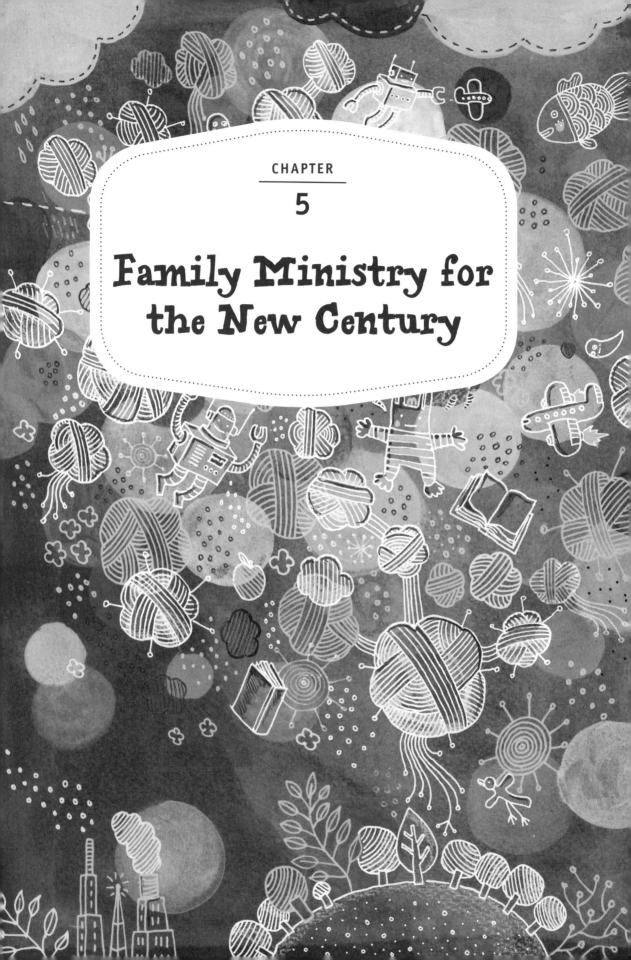

Family Ministry for the New Century

BUILT TO LAST

BY CARMEN KAMRATH

Family ministry is a challenge and an opportunity for churches today. Trends and research detail the need for ministry in this area, yet many churches experience difficulty defining the role family ministry should have in the church. It's no wonder when today's family structure itself is complicated and not easily defined. Couple this wide-open territory with the apprehension of an uncharted ministry frontier, and many churches opt to put family ministry on the back burner. And yet there's a sense of urgency in filling this gap. We're experiencing a generational shift in the 21st century—parents who value family time and are making every effort to make it a priority. Family ministry is a new frontier the church can't afford to leave uncharted.

THE NEW FAMILY STRUCTURE

What is a family? The answer to that question is complex in today's world. I recently attended an elementary school field trip to the zoo. During the one-hour bus ride, I met kids who came from the traditional family setting—mom, dad, siblings, and the family pet, all living in the same house. But I also met two boys who lived with their grandparents and a sweet girl living with a family who took her in when her biological parents went to jail. Another girl lived with her dad during the school year and her mom over the summer months. And then there was an outgoing little boy who told me he lived with two mommies.

Yes, today's family structure is complicated. Nearly 69 percent of American youth are living in nontraditional families, according to the Stepfamily Association. The 2000 U.S. Census Bureau of Household and Family Statistics has tracked the variety and growth of different family structures in recent years. Single parents account for 27 percent of family households. One out of every 25 children lives with neither parent. Also, 2.4 million grandparents are the primary caregivers for children today. The number of children living in households with unmarried partners has increased by 72 percent in the last decade. And the growth of interracial families, more than 4.5 million at the turn of the century, will likely continue to climb.

Biological roots have taken on a new meaning for many of today's families. Medical advances in fertility such as in vitro fertilization, surrogate births, and sperm banks have given couples and individuals options for starting a family. Some of these methods involve biological ties for children in which they may or may not continue to have a long-term relationship with the parent. Hollywood stars have created a heightened interest in adoption, and foreign borders are making the process easier for couples and individuals to adopt internationally.

The physical makeup of the family isn't the only change on the horizon. The value placed on the family unit is shifting as a new generation steps into the parenting role.

Labeled as slackers in their youth, Gen Xers are all grown up and shedding this reputation as they become parents. This generation is planning how they'll parent even before they get pregnant. The marketing research firm Reach Advisors revealed that Gen X parents place family first over careers. These young parents are happily accepting careers that allow for flexibility and predictability, even at the expense of lower salaries, if it means spending more time at home. Moms and dads share parenting responsibilities more than couples in previous generations did, including taking time off from their careers to be stay-at-home parents. Gen X parents embrace the return to traditional values and giving their children a sense of security at home. This generation enjoys spending time with its kids and wants to experience life with its children.

As generations collide, we're beginning to see the first of the Millennial generation step into the parenting role. Like Gen Xers, Millennials will choose a career that allows them to put family first. As this generation enters adulthood, its goals include being good parents and establishing a loving family environment. Early research has shown that this generation has an increased interest in family, spirituality, and community. These young adults have enjoyed a good relationship with their parents and are expected to continue to consult with them on major decisions. This relational shift will likely add a new element to child rearing, with multiple generations having a hand in the upbringing of children in the 21st century.

WHAT IS FAMILY MINISTRY?

The church is often described as a place where the spiritual needs of all individuals are met—from birth to the grave. Historically, the church has divided families as they walked through the door. It rarely offered programs that combined children and parents to learn and grow in their faith. On the other hand, new family ministries target the family unit, helping parents and children *together* grow in their relationship with each other and with God.

Psalm 78:1-7 reminds us how important it is to pass our faith to future generations—ministering to families is essential in supporting parents as spiritual teachers and mentors. As a church, we have only a limited time each week to influence kids in their faith journeys. Parents, on the other hand, have the home field advantage. Ministering to families is equipping parents for their God-given role in the home.

Family ministry is foundational in meeting the needs of the 21st-century family. A social shift in our society has placed a greater value on the needs of the family rather than the needs of the individual. The church can be a corner piece in implementing and supporting programs that fill this need. With two generations placing family time as one of the top priorities of parenthood, we can anticipate family ministry being one of the new catalysts for church growth.

Family Ministry Elements

It's time to build a ministry that has a lasting impact! Here are three key targets to focus on and use as a filter as you shape your family ministry.

- *Parent Support*—One of the primary goals of family ministry is to support parents in the important role of raising children. Many parents want to spend time with their kids. They have good intentions about talking to their kids on a deeper level. They want to share their faith. The problem is—they don't know how.

To get your family ministry to equip parents as they journey through parenthood, help parents learn how to discipline with love or talk to their children about sex by offering classes taught by experts in the field. Form small groups so parents can be a support for each other. Teach parents how to share their faith with their children, and assure them that they don't need to be a Bible scholar to do so. One of the most guilt-lifting moments for parents is when they realize it's OK to learn together and make Bible discoveries *with* their child. Give parents the resources to have faith discussions with their children by providing discussion starters and activities that go beyond the Sunday school classroom and into the home.

- *Family Support*—Parents and kids sometimes need a relationship jump-start. Provide opportunities for families to have fun together. Offer recreational classes such as pottery or building rockets. Plan field trips with family discounts to baseball games or the zoo. Host a board game night or a spaghetti dinner so families can socialize together. Family ministry can provide a valuable lesson in the art of having fun together.

Another essential component to family ministry is the opportunity for families to grow in their faith together. A family worship time that's kid-focused is a great way for children to share their style of music and activities with parents. Focus the teaching time of worship on what kids are learning in Sunday school to give parents a glimpse of what their children are learning. Offer classes where parents and children learn together on topics such as baptism or communion. Group's FaithWeaver® Bible Curriculum allows families to all study the same Bible stories at the same time. Provide experiential learning opportunities for families to make faith discoveries together such as a family VBS, like Group's HolyLand Adventure™ vacation Bible school, or a walk-through series of thematic learning stations.

Families grow deeper in their faith when they serve together. Community service opportunities bond families in a unique way. Serving meals to the homeless, planting a garden for an elderly resident, or cleaning up a local park allows parents and children to put their faith into action. Family ministries can provide opportunities for parents and children to reach out to others by teaching them to live out their faith.

- *Community Support*—Family ministries can step up and meet the needs of the community by providing outreach opportunities for families. Take a look at your community and identify where there are gaps. Here are some ideas for your family ministry to reach out to the community.

- *Parents' Night Out*—Provide a low-cost child-care service for parents to have a date night while their children are involved in a safe and structured program.

- *Support Groups*—Many families in crisis are required by law to attend a support group. Provide a room in your church for these groups, and offer participants information on your family ministry.

- *Help for Single Moms*—Sponsor a car-service day for single moms, complete with an oil change and fluid check—free of charge.

- *Adopt-a-Family*—Your family ministry can encourage church families to adopt a needy family by providing them with gifts and a meal over the holidays.

- *Sports Leagues*—If your community lacks kids' sports programs, your family ministry can fill the gap. Or offer an alternative league that stresses good sportsmanship and character education.

- *Family Events*—Offer large events for families that target the community at large but offer an opportunity for families to have fun together. A live Nativity at Christmas or a family-oriented concert is a great way to show the community that you care about families.

WHERE TO START

One of the biggest obstacles in establishing a family ministry is figuring out who oversees and owns the ministry. Does it fall under adult ministry or children's ministry? Or both? Does it mean hiring a new pastor to oversee the ministry? And how can family ministry be successful without infringing on the goals of other ministries?

Embarking on any new adventure is exciting, scary, and risky. It's important to start with prayer as the foundation for your new ministry. Pray for God's direction, for the ministry's vision, and for leaders to emerge.

Plant the Seed

One of the first roadblocks in starting a new ministry is church leadership. It's important for leaders to see the value in starting a family ministry.

- *Communicate*—Share your vision for family ministry and its potential as a growth component for your church. Give examples of how you plan to reach your community at large. Talk about the important role parents play in the spiritual growth of their children and how your ministry will equip them for success.

- *Have a Plan*—Where will you start? How will you communicate the need to others in your church and community? Who will provide leadership in this new ministry? What are your initial goals and your long-term goals? Anticipate questions and concerns and be ready with answers and an action plan.

- *Take Action*—Be ready for the green light and move without hesitation. As a children's ministry leader, you're in touch with the value of family ministry, so take the lead. Develop a staffing plan as the ministry grows. Discuss with church staff how family ministry can benefit and partner with other ministries. Have a timeline and targets to reach before you launch. Assemble a leadership team to help with planning and implementation.

The key is to help leaders envision your dream and capture your passion for this new adventure. Your enthusiasm for the ministry will be contagious.

Cultivate

The next step is sharing your vision with your church family. Some may be resistant and feel that family ministry doesn't meet their needs. The overwhelming majority (especially families!) will likely cheer and eagerly anticipate your ministry's launch. Use these ideas to prepare your congregation and introduce them to family ministry.

- *Warm Up*—Generate support for the ministry rather than applying pressure for involvement. Instill your intent to serve families, not burden them. Give your church members a glimpse of the need by showering them with ideas on how this ministry will benefit their family—both relationally and spiritually. Will you offer parenting classes? family worship? special events? family-oriented activities? Give examples of what the ministry will look like, and ask for input on what families hope to experience through this new ministry.

- *Accelerate*—Challenge your church to participate in this new ministry adventure. Survey the needs of your church and community. Get input from kids in your children's ministry. Invite people into roles of leadership and involvement. Host an information open house during your weekend services, and have families who are already onboard with your vision answer questions. Ask your pastor to have a sermon series on families. Set a target date to launch the ministry and build excitement and enthusiasm by giving regular updates to your congregation. Families will feel part of the ministry from the start if they're in the information loop.

- *Launch*—Sometimes it's better to start small and achieve success and excellence. Your first family ministry opportunity should reflect the ministry's vision and goals. Determine what kind of family programming is a good fit for your church and community and start there. It may be a workshop for parents on discipline, a family picnic, or a baby dedication service. Make it a goal to show parents genuine support—give them helpful tools such as a family devotion idea, parenting tips, or the gift of time with their children. The launch of your family ministry needs to communicate a reassurance of your goal to support, equip, and love parents and children.

Feels Like Home

A challenge that will weigh on family ministry in the 21st century will be to help the growing number of nontraditional families feel part of the larger church community. Help all families feel part of your greater church family with these simple reminders.

- *Roll Out the Welcome Mat*—Nontraditional families tend to stay away from church for fear of feeling like outsiders. Help families feel welcome with a sincere attitude. Nontraditional families are on high alert and won't come back if a church is quick to pass judgment or tries to fix their unique situation. Reach out to families by including them in all church activities, and remember that they may not feel invited to a program unless you extend an invitation. Don't always separate families into groups such as single parents or interracial families. There are times when ministry to a specific group is appropriate, but making a habit of segregation will never build community. Gather input from all families on ideas that meet their needs and how your church family can be a support for parents and children.

- *A Comfy Couch*—When you're a guest in someone's home, nothing feels better than sitting on a couch that embraces you with comfort. Nontraditional families will feel at home when a church isn't hypersensitive to their differences. Help grandparents raising grandchildren feel part of your ministry by including them in a class on discipline, rather than assuming that they've "been there, done that." Stay-at-home dads like to be included in play groups, and uncles or male family friends should be able to come to a Dads and Daughters Dinner without encountering a thousand questions.

- *Keep the Porch Light On*—Families may be very involved in your ministry and then disappear for a time. The nontraditional family can have unique needs that the church must be sensitive to. Follow up with families who have dropped off the radar by extending help and resources when they're going through a difficult time. Families will feel like part of the greater church community when they're enthusiastically welcomed back from a hiatus. Like the son who strayed and was lost, the church needs to be that welcoming father when families return home.

MINISTRY THAT LASTS

Family ministry has the unique quality of building a legacy. As children learn the importance of family and travel on a journey of faith with their parents, you plant a seed. This generation of parents, the parental pilgrims of the 21st century, have set the precedent that families are important. Family ministry cultivates that value and adds the nurturing element of a loving God who embraces parents and children. These are the roots that children of the 21st century will carry on to future generations.

Try This

BY DANA WILKERSON

FAMILY TALENT SHOW

Use this activity to explore with families what it says in Romans 12:6a: "In his grace, God has given us different gifts for doing certain things well."

Provide families the opportunity to spend time together, work together, and display each other's talents and gifts by staging a Family Talent Show! Each entry should include at least two family members, but encourage families to include as many family members as possible.

To promote variety among the acts, have families look at what they do best. Maybe one family has some talented artists, and they can ask audience members to give them directions on making a group painting right there onstage. Or perhaps another family loves basketball and can put on a Harlem Globetrotters-type show. And if a family is great at hospitality, they could show the audience how to set an inviting, family-friendly table, or they could make a fun fruit salad to share with everybody. Encourage creativity!

Instead of voting for the best performance, bring each family back up on stage for cheers and applause. For added fun, give each family a silly "trophy" related to their performance. (You'll need to know what they're doing beforehand to do this.) For example, if a family does a dance number, present them with a child's tutu. However you decide to celebrate, have fun!

Discuss Within Families:

- **What was the best moment you had while you were preparing for the talent show?**
- **What is one way you can use this family talent again?**

Activity 2

EVER CONSIDER ADOPTION?

(Scripture: Psalm 68:6a)

Have you ever moved far from home and had to make new friends and build a new "family"? There are probably many people in your church who are starved for family-type relationships. Consider college students, young couples who have just moved to the area, retirees who are living far from kids and grandkids, and single adults of any age. Hook them up with families in the church who can become their adoptive families.

Encourage families to include their new adopted family members in family events and celebrations, invite them to the kids' soccer games and band concerts, and take hikes together. It's also important that the involvement go both ways. Both lifestyles should be accepted, celebrated, and shared. When the young single buys his or her first house, the entire "family" can help with moving, repairs, painting, and so on. The retired grandma might love cooking a big meal for her adopted family and hosting them at her house for a game night.

A word of advice: These relationships might not always work out. Don't force it. Sometimes different personalities just don't click. When this happens, leave it up to the participants to decide what to do. Just let them know you're open to listen and give advice if "family" relationships get hard.

Bonus Idea

This is also a great opportunity for mentoring relationships to emerge. The 70-year-old retired man has much wisdom he can impart to a 30-year-old dad struggling to balance family and work. A middle-aged couple with teenage kids can be great mentors to the young couple expecting their first child.

Activity 3

FAMILY GROUPS

When families walk into your church on Sunday mornings, does each family member head in a different direction? If so, consider starting a family group ministry where all family members stay together. This can be implemented in several different ways.

You can match up similar-type families. Instead of having a small group just for young couples, have a small group for young families—including the kids. Or mix things up a lot and create small groups that include people in different stages of life. Maybe one group includes a family with three teenagers, a 30-something single, a retired couple, and a single dad with a couple of young kids.

It's up to you (and your pastor or Sunday school director or church board, or whoever needs to be included in these kinds of decisions) to decide what will work best in your church. Maybe you'll decide to have the entire church do this long-term, or it might be something some church members voluntarily try during the summers. You make the call!

After a month or so, check in with the participants to see how things are going. Ask questions such as these:

- **Have you spent time with any of the other families in your group outside of church? If so, what did you do?**
- **If Jesus were to participate with your family group, what is one comment he would make about it?**
- **What is one thing you can personally do to make your family group better?**

Activity 4

"LEARN FROM OTHERS' MISTAKES" NIGHT

"As a dog returns to its vomit, so a fool repeats his foolishness." Proverbs 26:11—Kids find this verse intriguing!

How do we learn best? The hard way—from our own mistakes. How can we try to avoid that painful process? We can learn from others' mistakes! Have a Parents' Night Out at your church, but make it so much more than just a night away from the kids. And you know what? You don't have to just invite parents! Invite all adults—they'll all get a kick out of it.

Here's what you do. Plan a fun night for the adults with lots of food, lots of fun, and lots of time to share. If you have time, you might want to consider watching a funny parenting movie like *Cheaper by the Dozen* (PG) to kick things off. The whole point of the evening is for the parents to share their "horror stories" of parenting. Encourage each parent or couple to share a time when he or she really screwed up. After the groans and laughs subside, encourage interaction where the storytellers and others can talk about what they did to patch things up or could have done to avoid that situation then and avoid it in the future.

Have participants discuss these questions in small groups:

- **Which story would your kids say could've been about your family? Why?**
- **Who would you like to talk to in more depth about his or her story? Why?**
- **What did you learn tonight that you'll put into practice?**

Copyright Laws

Movie clips under three minutes are technically covered under the fair use doctrine (which allows portions of a work to be exhibited for educational purposes). But to be on the safe side, you can obtain a license for a small fee from Christian Video Licensing International. Visit www.cvli.org for more information. (You can't charge admission to a function where you screen clips.)

Activity 5

GARAGE SALE GIVEAWAY!

Matthew 25:35 says, "For I was hungry and you fed me. I was thirsty, and you gave me a drink." Use this activity to refresh your neighbors, literally!

A summer tradition in many areas is the town-wide or neighborhood garage sale. You can use these events to give families the opportunity to spend time together, serve their neighbors, and meet new people!

When one of these community events happens, organize families that live in that area to serve their neighbors by giving away free drinks and snacks. Have them load up a cart or wagon with their refreshments and take it around the neighborhood. Encourage not just service but interaction with the families holding the garage sales and the patrons. A little friendliness and service can go a long way toward building new relationships!

Bonus Idea

Encourage families to participate in the garage sales themselves. Perhaps a couple of families can put their items together at one house. Then they can use the proceeds to donate to a local charity or to a family going through a hard time.

Activity 6

CREATE-YOUR-OWN WHATEVER

At home, families will create something together related to an activity they enjoy doing together. If they enjoy playing games, they can create their own one-of-a-kind game. If they enjoy music, they can write a song together. If they enjoy hiking, they can make walking sticks. I think you get the picture.

Once the creations have been completed, have the families share them with others. You might want to have an exhibition/performance night at church so all the families can share their creations with the whole church.

Family Discussion:

- **Was it hard or easy to come up with something you all enjoy doing? Why?**
- **What is another idea you saw tonight that your family would also enjoy?**
- **If you were to do this again, what would you do?**

Activity 7

DAY TRIP PLANNING EVENT

Invite families to gather at church to plan personalized day trips. Ask them to bring maps, travel books, and whatever else they might have that will help them and others plan a trip. If possible, you might want to set up some computers with Internet access.

To begin, have families share stories of some of their best day trips in the area. When they finish, help families start planning a future trip for their own family (or group of families). They can get ideas from others' trips, travel guides, maps, and possibly the Internet. Encourage all family members to participate and offer ideas for activities. Families will have to work together to come up with a plan that includes places or activities that suit everyone.

Bonus Idea

As families share about previous trips, guide each family to create a scrapbook page with photos and descriptions of a favorite day trip. (You'll need to ask them to bring pictures along, and you'll need to provide scrapbook pages and scrapbooking materials.) Then combine these pages into a book—adding pages yearly—so that all families in the church can access ideas as they plan family vacations.

Family Discussion:

- **What made planning this trip different from planning other family trips?**
- **Did you learn anything about a family member's creativity or planning abilities? Who? In what way?**
- **If you decided to plan an African safari vacation, which family member would do which part of the planning? Why?**

Activity 8

FIFTH SUNDAY FAMILY WORSHIP

You'll need the cooperation of your pastor, worship leader, and other church leaders for this one, but it'll be worth it!

Each time there's a fifth Sunday in a month, make the worship service very family-friendly. Encourage families to all sit together. If extended families are present, invite all of them to sit together. Make sure the music is kid-friendly and there is opportunity for the kids to move around and/or wiggle, and tell the preacher to keep the sermon short!

This service will show families that you value them and support them.

Bonus Idea

Include kids in leading the service. Perhaps a young pianist can play a prelude or a young singer can lead a worship song. Consider putting the youth group in charge of announcements, or have a young person say the closing prayer. Include the children however you can.

Activity 9

KAZAK-WHO?

Read Matthew 28:18-20 and Acts 1:8. God wants us to share his love to the whole world!

How many countries are there in the world? How many people groups are there in the world? We could give you the answer to those questions, but what fun is that? Let the church families help with the answers. Challenge each family to "adopt" a country or people group they don't know much about or perhaps have never even heard of. For help finding these countries and people groups, go to:

- www.peoplegroups.org
- www.joshuaproject.net
- www.gmi.org/ow

Once families have made their choices, there's no limit to what they can do. They may want to put up maps and pictures in their houses, research about their chosen people, eat food from the adopted culture, and pray for the people of that country or group. You can help connect families with missions agencies that can hook them up with missionaries in their adopted areas that they can write to, pray for, financially support, and possibly even visit. Let the families decide how far they want to go (figuratively and literally) in this activity.

Family Discussion:

- **What did you like most about learning about how people from other countries live?**
- **Why is it important to learn about other cultures?**
- **How can we continue learning about and sharing God's love with people from other places?**

Activity 10

HEAR, O ISRAEL!

Deuteronomy 6:6-7 says, "Commit yourselves wholeheartedly to these commands that I am giving you today. Repeat them again and again to your children. Talk about them when you are at home and when you are on the road, when you are going to bed and when you are getting up."

How many hours a week do you have the kids at church? One? Two? How many hours do their parents have them? Lots more than you do! They have much more time with their kids to model and shape their beliefs and actions. And yes, the Bible actually says that parents are to teach their own kids about God! One snag with that, though—some parents don't understand how to do it. So why don't you help them?

You'll need lots of help with this, but it will be well worth it for the parents and their kids. Find people who are willing and able to lead classes that will teach parents how to teach their kids at home. They might need help with Bible study, mentoring, modeling, and just living life in a way that teaches their kids who God is and how he wants us to live our lives as Christians. In fact, why not just ask parents what they want help with, and go from there!

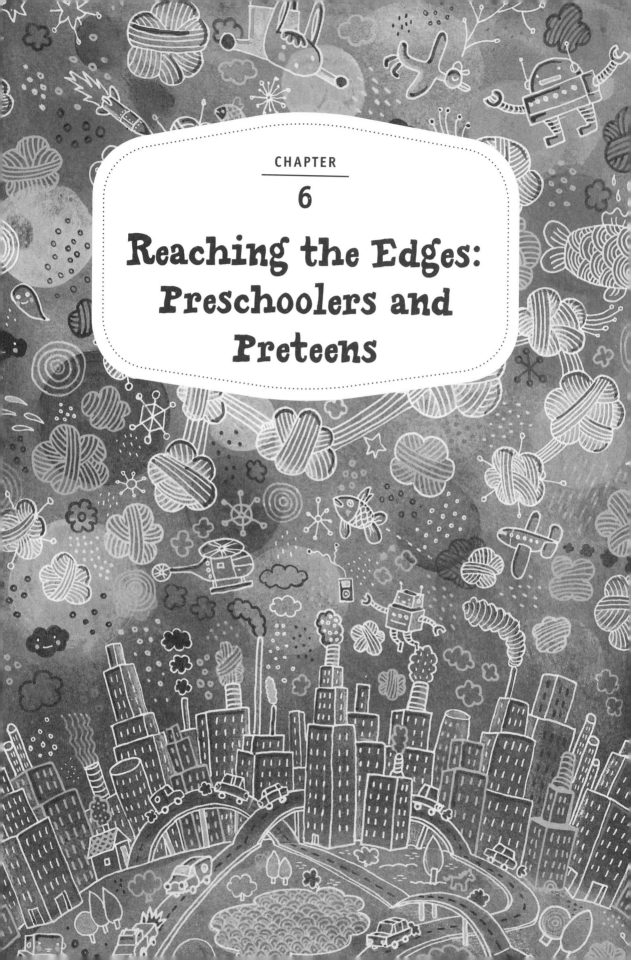

CHAPTER

6

Reaching the Edges: Preschoolers and Preteens

REACHING THE NEXT GENERATION OF PRESCHOOLERS

BY SONDRA SAUNDERS

WHERE WE'VE BEEN

It's a half-hour until "go time"—the time when kids arrive for Sunday school. As you walk down the hall, you glance appreciatively at the bulletin board that welcomes little ones to your children's ministry. You love the way you've decorated that board—which is why you haven't changed it in over a year. You peek into a nearby classroom and note with satisfaction that the flannel board is propped on an easel, faithfully awaiting its cardboard characters. Uh-oh! A lion's head is on the floor—why won't that tape hold? You deftly reattach the paper parts and set the worn lion between Daniel and King Darius in the easel tray.

Eventually your volunteers show up, and you notice (once again) that you'll have to improvise since two of them were unable to make it this morning. But that might not be a problem anyway, since the stream of kids that began 10 minutes ago has already ebbed to a trickle. Attendance has waned, but you don't know why.

WHERE WE'RE GOING

Reading this book is a sign that you're interested in the trend toward a relevant, energized children's ministry that speaks to kids where they are. You probably understand that the *way* we teach is just as important as *what* we teach in order to guide children in an authentic relationship with Jesus. And for some of us in leadership roles, this means a dramatic shift in educational philosophy. Change—even when positive and rewarding—can be unsettling, but thank you for caring enough to risk discomfort for the sake of the children you shepherd. You'll find that understanding new trends will not only enhance your children's ministry, but it'll also energize you and your staff. Consider the advice and adopt some of the ideas within these pages, and watch as the trickle of attendance swells to a steady flow!

WHO *ARE* THESE KIDS ANYWAY?

In terms of generational trends, we're now welcoming the Homelander Generation (born from 2003 to the present) into our preschool classrooms. They are surrounded by entertainment and will be more techno-savvy than any generation yet. They will also be used to choice, having had so many resources and so much information at their fingertips. Strauss and Howe, in *Millenials Rising: The Next Great Generation,* predict that the next generation will be "sensitive and complex social technicians, advocates of fair play and the politics of inclusion." They'll also "become sensitive helpmates, lending their expertise and cooperation to an era of growing social calm." These characteristics directly affect the way these children learn, which directly affects ways to teach.

Physically speaking, kids themselves have changed over the years. Today it's considered irresponsible, not generous, to blithely offer syrupy juices or sweet cookies for snacks. The trend in children's ministry to promote healthfulness must follow suit. Along those lines, parents desire an environment for their children that promotes exercise and active play—and kids prefer it, too. Less lecture and more active learning in the classroom isn't only the easiest solution, but it also increases the likelihood that children will remember what the lesson was about.

WELCOME...WITH WHIMSY

Many parents of preschoolers will choose a church (or choose whether to attend church at all) based upon the resources it offers their children. What are they looking for? Likely the same thing they'd notice when searching for a potential day-care or preschool facility: a winning first impression. Kids want color and a fun, playful atmosphere—so do their parents. A word of caution here: Sensory overload is a bygone trend. The learning environment isn't necessarily optimal when walls are smothered with posters, quotations, charts, and trinkets, and when ceilings are hung with...whatever will dangle from a string. Today we realize that relevance—not clutter—matters, even to a toddler.

And the way we teach includes more than lesson content—environment plays an important role, especially for babies and toddlers. Offer a safe, warm embrace; a room of bright colors, engaging music, or pleasant aromas that stimulate the senses; and even a greeting of familiar puppets who communicate the message, "We're glad you're here!" You'll create an atmosphere that preschoolers will long associate with God's love. And since preschoolers are already forming their impressions of God (and church), we can't afford *not* to appeal to their senses.

In response to emerging trends in both education and entertainment, churches have a unique opportunity to be ultra-creative. How about a twisting slide that transports little ones from the registration table to their large group area? What if kids were greeted by life-sized stuffed animals—that talk? Changes needn't be drastic or costly, though. Some churches have painstakingly (and lovingly) designed their children's area thematically with vibrant colors and whimsical scenes, choosing a different theme for each age group. Even smaller churches can do this—it's amazing how a roll or two of wallpaper and a bolt of fabric can transform a room. The trend is to "think like a child" when decorating for preschoolers. Take a tour of your preschool area—sitting in a wagon. Look at the decorations, toys, and views from your children's vantage point. Select small furniture. Use big pillows. Arrange pictures at a child's eye level. Include "stations" around the room that are set up to accommodate many learning styles. Above all: Let the room's décor shout "Welcome!" to children and their parents.

THE TECHNO TREND

We can't deny it—today's preschoolers are captivated by the screen: whether it is a TV show, a video game, a computer monitor, a portable DVD player, or even a cell phone. What does this mean to your church? While we don't necessarily want to "compete," we do need to keep up.

For example, our church provides a Web site dedicated to children's ministry. On it, parents can find information about upcoming events, needs for volunteers, biographies of our staff, and program descriptions. We've also included a page about kids with special needs. Preschoolers can access games, coloring pages, devotionals, and Bible stories. The purpose of this site is two-fold: It provides parents and kids with news they need, and it can serve as an outreach. If the trend is for kids to go online, our church will greet them there.

Kids' expectations may have changed over the years, but we can rest on this comforting fact: God remains consistent. Bible truths are the same as they always were—what's changed is the way we deliver those truths to the kids. If we're deliberate and purposeful in the way we use technology to tell God's story, we haven't altered his story at all—we've only altered the vehicle for telling it. Imagine how Daniel's plight in the lions' den would come to life for preschoolers in a darkened room with the dingy walls of a prison den projected on a screen. Suddenly, the silence is punctuated by ferocious roars of hungry lions! But here's the filter: The means of telling the story must enhance its content, not detract from it. A showing of the cartoon *The Lion King* isn't going to do much to further preschoolers' understanding of God's faithfulness to Daniel, for example. And if the vehicle itself becomes the focal point, or if it proves to be distracting, it's not a suitable means for teaching. In other words, not all text on a PowerPoint slide needs to swirl or melt or explode, and lessons shouldn't be conveyed through single-participant computer games. While the use of technology is certainly a teaching trend, it is one to use with purpose.

SAFEKEEPING

An unavoidable trend in children's ministry includes "the three S's": screening, safety, and security. General needs for precaution as well as specific family situations have necessitated a closer hold on the preschoolers in our care. For this reason, your children's ministry must:

- **Screen your volunteers by performing nationwide background checks on all staff.** Personally interview each potential employee or volunteer.

- **Promote safety.** Check equipment and playground apparatus frequently for sharp edges and broken pieces. Sanitize every toy after each session, and clean all beds thoroughly. Be aware of the items kids bring to your classroom, and develop a policy, if necessary, that keeps personal toys or other belongings at home.

- **Provide security.** Depending upon the size of your church, it may actually be necessary to use a system as thorough as a badge check for parents to pick up their children. Smaller churches can often rely on recognition. Also, perform a head count before the class leaves the room together and upon its return.

This area of children's ministry can appear to be a dichotomy. We want the church to communicate a message of warmth and welcome, but at the same time we're responsible for the cherished lives in our care. Security measures needn't be harsh or impersonal. As with anything else, a genuine smile offered along with the request for identification is always a good way to soften the situation.

KEEPING IT REAL

Let's assume that your preschool ministry is onboard with all emerging trends. Your classrooms are engaging and inviting. You're using cutting-edge technology to give dimension and flair to Bible stories and object lessons. Your meeting areas are safe, secure, and they reflect a healthy environment. What's left? Relevance. Kids of the Homelander Generation expect it. Even babies will benefit from it. It really doesn't matter whether we're in lock step with current trends if we don't help kids understand this: Jesus is relevant. He's real, he's accessible, and they can apply his truths to their lives.

This is where *people* come in—volunteers who model God's love for children. Repeated affirmations such as "God is so glad you came today, and so am I!" or "Jesus is your friend, and I am, too!" are not lost on toddlers. They'll more readily understand a benevolent God when they view his church as an accepting and caring family. And to a preschooler, the Sunday school room *is* church!

PRAISE GOD!

One thing we'll surely do in heaven is worship together, but let's not wait—let's start today! We now understand that even preschoolers can be taught the relevance of worship. Worship is praise and singing—it's an expression of devotion to God. And the emotions they experience when they praise at such a young age are foundational for their developing Christian walk. Familiarize children with actions and responses of worship so they'll feel comfortable participating with their families in church and so they'll understand what's going on. As you'll discover in this book, family ministries are emerging—and with it, family worship.

KNOW...THEN GO

You've already laid the groundwork for a preschool ministry dedicated to helping kids grow in their relationship with Jesus. But for your ministry to be vibrant and impactful, it's important to stay abreast of change. Study the trends in society at large. Understand today's culture so you'll understand what's relevant to kids. That doesn't mean tossing out tradition—instead, *build* on tradition as you explore new ways to lead children to God. And if it helps to take baby steps, start with the bulletin board.

Try This

BY BECKI MANNI

WELCOME!

An exciting trend in children's ministry is the inclusion of babies in lessons. We're finally recognizing how much they internalize and build upon, and we now understand the positive association they make about church even at this young age.

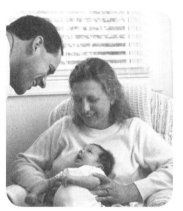

To involve toddlers in the lesson, have them sit in a circle. If you're in a nursery, have volunteers hold babies in their laps. Open with a simple prayer, thanking God for bringing his precious little ones to Sunday school to hear about him.

Sing a welcome song that kids will recognize, moving from child to child as you sing and hug each one in the circle. Depending on children's ages, they'll begin to react after two or three weeks of hearing the same song. Babies will babble, sway, bang the table, or simply attend closely. Toddlers will sing along. And all will sit up and take notice when it's their turn to receive a hug!

Welcome new children to your class by giving each one a sticker or paper crown to wear, or maybe even cloth streamers to wave.

"Welcome Song"
(Sung to the tune of "Are You Sleeping?")

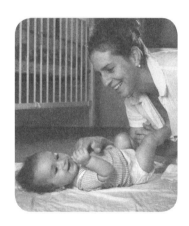

God bless [child's name]; God bless [child's name].
God made you; God made you.
We are glad you came; we are glad you came.
God bless you; God bless you.

Activity 2

WE LOVE THE BIBLE!

Help children connect God with the Bible. Gather them in a circle, and as you sing one of the following songs, have children either pat or hug a Bible and then pass it to the next child. If there are babies in your circle, have volunteers cradle the babies in their laps as they pass the Bible.

"We Love the Bible"
(Sung to the tune of "Mary Had a Little Lamb")

Babies:
We love to pat the Bi-ble, Bi-ble, Bi-ble,
We love to pat the Bi-ble
Because it is God's Word.

Toddlers:
We love to hug the Bi-ble, Bi-ble, Bi-ble,
We love to hug the Bi-ble
Because it is God's Word.

Preschool:
We love to read the Bi-ble, Bi-ble, Bi-ble,
We love to read the Bi-ble
Because it is God's Word.

Activity 3

JESUS LOVES US

While children are gathered in a circle, use hand or finger puppets to tell the story of Jesus' love for children. (Keep in mind that babies and toddlers may be frightened of puppets bigger than they are.)

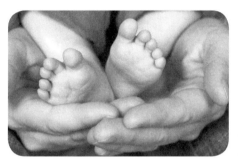

Open your Bible to Mark 10:13, and tell the children of Jesus' special love for them. Don't read straight from the Bible, but paraphrase in very basic terms—even to babies. It's enough to simply tell them that Jesus loves them very much, and even better to incorporate that truth into a song. For example, "Jesus Loves Us" is sung to a familiar tune, and it can be personalized for each child:

"Jesus Loves Us"
(Sung to the tune of "Are You Sleeping?")

> We love Jesus; we love Jesus.
> Yes, we do; yes, we do!
> Jesus loves [child's name]; Jesus loves [child's name].
> Yes, he does; yes, he does!
> Jesus loves you; Jesus loves you.
> Yes, he does; yes, he does!
> He will love you always; he will love you always.
> Yes, he will; yes, he will!

Remember, babies can learn that Jesus loves them! Using a plastic-edged crib mirror, show each child's reflection as you sing his or her name in "Jesus Loves Us." They'll also respond if you guide their hands through simple signing or hand motions as they sing, or if you use "comfort toys" such as a small stuffed lamb that squeaks.

Even before they can talk, toddlers can participate in story "follow-ups." Ask short, concrete questions related to that day's activities, and respond with exaggerated physical motions. Because lessons should be repetitive, or at least overlap in content, children will anticipate the questions and react with the physical answers. Non-speakers will show the big action while talkers will act out the motions and offer answers.

For example, ask:

Who loves Jesus? Raise your arms in the air and shout, "We do!"

Who does Jesus love? Wrap your arms across your chest and shout, "Me!"

Where is Jesus' story? Clap your hands together and shout, "The Bible!"

To guide the very young toddlers in responses to questions about feelings, it's OK to model responses. For example, if you ask "How does that make me feel?" you might hop up and down and say, "Happy!"

Familiarize babies and toddlers with the concept of talking to God by ending each time together with a short one- or two-sentence prayer. Thank God for the chance to learn about him, and bless the children. If toddlers can talk, have them repeat your simple prayer a few words at a time.

Activity 4

JESUS' LOVE

Use every opportunity to reinforce the lesson that Jesus loves them when children are in your classroom or nursery. It's easy to incorporate this into play and into any activity in the room. For example, you have a baby's undivided attention during changing, so why not ask, "Who loves [baby's name]?" and wiggle baby's legs or arms as you respond, "Jesus loves [baby's name]!" Or guide children in conversations about the lesson while they're playing with the toys or out on the playground.

In this version of "London Bridge," toddlers acknowledge that Jesus loves them as they play—the bridge becomes a way to "catch" the one Jesus loves! Or babies can enjoy the lyrics and melody as you rock them while singing the song.

"Jesus Loves Me; Yes, He Does"
(Sung to the tune of "London Bridge")

Jesus loves me; yes, he does;
Yes, he does; yes, he does.
Jesus loves me; yes, he does.
He's my friend!

Movements

Two preschoolers form a bridge by facing each other, clasping each other's hands, and holding them high enough for other children to pass through. During the beginning of each verse, all children skip, one by one, underneath the bridge. At "He's my friend," the "bridge" comes down to encircle the child passing through.

Play until each toddler has had a chance to be "caught" by Jesus' love.

Activity 5

GOD MADE EVERYTHING!

Teach preschoolers that God made everything, but break "everything" into small, simple categories that you'll repeat for several weeks. Remember, repetition is key in learning at this age! And to really engage children, include objects they can touch or play with.

For example, a lesson about how God created us could include a baby doll. Use the doll to teach about our arms, legs, eyes, and ears. Ask children to point these out on the doll and then to find their own arms, legs, eyes, nose, and so on. At this age they like to play "Show me your nose," or "Show me your ears," or "Wiggle your fingers."

Say: **God made your eyes so you can see how much he loves you. Blink your eyes!**

God made your ears so you can hear how much he loves you. Cup your ears as though listening, and have children do the same.

God made your tongue so you can taste how much he loves you. Point to your tongue!

God made your nose so you can smell how much he loves you. Wiggle your nose!

Play several times using different body parts and repeating the body parts you began with.

Sing "Head and Shoulders, Knees and Toes" or "The Hokey Pokey" while physically wiggling each of those parts. Reinforce that God made us and that God loves us just the way we are. Toddlers aren't too young to learn that God made each of us to be unique.

Ask:

• **Who made you?** (Say, "God did!")

• **Who loves you?** (Say, "God does!")

• **Who made your toes?** (Say, "God did! Now let's wiggle them!")

• **Who made your hands?** (Say, "God did! Now let's clap them!")

Activity 6

OBEDIENCE

God wants us to obey. Nursery or toddler years may seem too early to begin teaching about abstract ideas such as obedience, sharing, and kindness. But presented in simple terms, these ideas can be taught just as you might teach about the love of Jesus—through repetition and familiarization.

A great way to do this is to link abstract concepts to actual stories. Children can learn about obedience as they relate it to Noah—he obeyed God by building the ark. You can also use the story of Adam and Eve to teach about obedience. They weren't obeying God when they ate the fruit.

Children can sing about obedience or act out the concept with hand motions. Don't exclude babies in the nursery—sing to them and guide their arms and legs in gentle movement.

"Obey Jesus"
(Sung to the tune of "Are You Sleeping?")

Obey Mommy; obey Daddy.
Yes, I do; yes, I do!
God says to obey; God says to obey.
Yes, he does; yes, he does.
Obey Jesus; obey Jesus.
Yes, I will; yes, I will.
He will love me always; he will love me always.
Yes, he will; yes, he will!

Activity 7

STOP AND PRAY

Preschoolers have an unwavering faith, and they aren't too young to learn that God listens when they pray. They are capable of praying and believing God for answers. Use this lesson to encourage children to pray many times in their day.

Put these items in a large box with a lid that closes:

- a clear plastic bag with a cup and plastic silverware sealed inside (helping)
- a small pillow (sleepy)
- a tablecloth (hungry/eating)
- a small toy car (stuck in the car)
- something with a smiley face on it (happy)
- a fun toy (playing)
- a stuffed lion or other scary animal (scared)

Gather children in a circle around the box, and ask them to tell you about times when they pray. Open the box and let children take turns pulling an item out of the box and telling about what it reminds them of. Ask them if they can talk with God at each of those times. Read aloud 1 Thessalonians 5:17.

Say: **Jesus wants us to talk with him all of the time!** Ask children to name other times when they could talk to God. Ask them to help you sing this action song to the tune of "London Bridge." Have the children stand in their circle and show how they act in each situation. At the end of each verse, have the children take a jump to their right.

"I Will Pray"
(Sung to the tune of "London Bridge")

I will pray when I am sad,
I am sad,
I am sad.
I will pray when I am sad.
God will listen!

Insert these words for other verses: glad, hurt, mad, scared, helping, playing, hungry, sleepy, stuck (in the car).

Gather children together and talk about how God will listen to us and take care of us. God takes care of the flowers and the birds. God says we are far more important to him than even the little sparrows. How much more will God take care of us (Psalm 84; Matthew 6)? Have children play the "Scatter, Sparrows!" game. Have children find a partner and tell their partner, "God will take care of you more than a sparrow!" Then ask the children to follow these directions: "Touch feet," "Touch wings," and "Tweet to your partner." Then call out, "Scatter, sparrows!" Have the children flap their wings and hurry to find a new partner, repeating, "God will take care of you more than a sparrow!" Repeat the directions in various orders several times, and then ask the children to help you answer these questions.

Ask:

- **Why will God take care of you?**
- **When can you talk with God about what you need?**

Take some time to let the children pray aloud. End by singing their new song, this time flapping their wings and flying to a new place after each verse.

Activity 8

JESUS DOES GREAT THINGS

Help preschoolers learn about one of Jesus' many miracles.

Use jump ropes to form two circular "fishnets" on the floor on opposite sides of the room. Choose two children to be fishermen, and say:

Jesus had many friends who were fishermen. Jesus called them disciples. They caught lots of fish, and then they sold the fish in the market for people to eat.

Let's play a game about fish. When I call out, "Big fish, little fish, swim, swim, swim!" everyone will run from the fishermen. If a fisherman touches you, go stand inside one of the fishnets. When the nets get too crowded, I'll call out, "Big fish, little fish, swim away free!" then you can all escape and play again. Play several times, changing fishermen each time.

Have all of the children sit in one of the fishnets and tell them the story of the disciples' miraculous catch of fish from Luke 5:1-11. Ask the children these questions:

- **Why do you think Jesus helped the fishermen catch all those fish?**
- **How do you think the fishermen felt when they caught all those fish?**

Tell the story again, helping the children act out the part of the fishermen (offering Jesus their boats, listening to Jesus talk, rowing their boats, tossing out their nets, pulling in their nets full of fish, leaving their nets to follow Jesus). Ask these questions:

- **What would you do if you were one of the fishermen?**
- **If you could ask Jesus one question about this story, what would it be?**

Play the "Fish" game again, allowing new children to be the fishermen.

Activity 9

GATHERING SHEEP

You'll need cotton balls and a rolled-up newspaper sheet for each student for this activity that will help preschool children understand how important they are to Jesus.

Scatter a package of cotton balls on the floor all over the room. Be sure there are at least five cotton balls for every child. Give every child a rolled newspaper tube. Ask children to stand in one place along the wall that will be their "sheep pen." Tell them to gather five of the "sheep" into their pen by "sweeping" them with their tubes. Play until everyone has his or her sheep safely in the pen, helping children count their sheep as they collect them.

When children have collected their sheep, ask them to sit with their sheep and answer these questions:

- **What was the hardest part about this game?**
- **Would the game be harder if the cotton balls were real baby sheep? Why?**

Tell the story of the lost sheep from Luke 15:3-7. Ask:

- **Why do you think the man would leave all of his sheep to find one that was lost?**
- **Why would the man have a party to celebrate that he found the lost sheep?**
- **If Jesus cares more about you than he does about sheep, will he come looking for you when you are lost? Why do you think so?**

Ask children to take turns telling the story to a partner. Then let children play the game again or take turns hiding their cotton balls for a partner to find. Encourage the children to take their cotton balls home and play a hiding game with their family and tell their family the story of the missing sheep. Let children practice telling the story to a partner before leaving.

Activity 10

JESUS, MY INVISIBLE SUPERHERO

Help preschoolers to understand the difference between pretend superheroes and our real superhero, Jesus. All you need are facial tissues to help them "see" what they cannot "see."

Ask children to tell you about their favorite superheroes. Ask them to answer these questions:

- **What can this superhero do?**
- **Is this superhero pretend or real? How do you know?**
- **Could Jesus be a superhero? Why or why not?**

Give children a facial tissue, and ask them to toss it in the air and then try to keep it in the air by blowing it. Ask:

- **What kept your facial tissue in the air?**
- **Is the air real or pretend? How do you know?**

Explain that Jesus is real and superheroes are not. Superheroes are pretend people or people pretending on TV. Jesus was a real person who walked and talked to other real people. He said he would always be with us, even though we can't see him—just like we can't see the air that keeps the facial tissue up. Ask:

- **How can you tell your friends that Jesus is the only real superhero?**

Let children play with their facial tissues and give their explanations to each other. Then challenge them to go home and explain to their family and friends why Jesus is a real superhero.

REACHING—AND KEEPING —TODAY'S PRETEENS

BY TY BRYANT

no·mad *n.* 1. A member of a group of people who have no fixed home and move according to the seasons from place to place in search of food, water, and grazing land. 2. A person with no fixed residence who roams about; a wanderer.

When I think of preteens, the word *nomad* comes to mind. Imagine a group of people walking around, looking for a home, but unable to find a place where they *fit in*—a place where they're accepted for who they are and where they happen to be along life's journey. Preteens and early adolescents, by that description, seem to be a nomadic population—at least socially and emotionally. That's why I feel it's absolutely vital that the church of the 21st century focus on the preteen age group through intentional ways, such as hiring staff specifically called to minister to them and planning ministries and discipleship uniquely targeted to meet their needs.

I'm excited about the movement I see in churches to put more resources and staffing toward reaching—and keeping—fourth-, fifth-, and sixth-grade students involved in the local body of Christ. I truly believe (and have seen) that if you capture the hearts of preteen students for Jesus, there's a much higher retention rate of these students in the church, and more kids are enthused about making a difference for the kingdom.

Before looking at current trends in preteen ministry to discuss what "works," consider the characteristics of our current generation of preteens. If we desire to lead this current generation of preteens to a true relationship with a living God, we must understand them and the uniqueness they bring to the table.

A George Barna study reveals that 43 percent of all Americans who accept Jesus Christ as Savior do so before the age of 13. In other words, nearly half of all conversions in the United States happen before one's teenage years. Consider this: Children between the ages of 5 and12 in the United States number about 31 million—nearly the population of the entire state of California. Also consider that during these preteen years, lifelong habits, values, beliefs, and attitudes are formed. For that reason, it's extremely important that we intentionally construct a portion of our church staff, ministries, and activities to specifically reach these students.

Our current generation of preteens isn't easily moved or surprised. I say this because the average 8- to 13-year-old spends 48 hours per week either watching TV, playing video games, listening to music, going to the movies, working on the computer (going online), and/or engaging in some kind of mass media. The Internet is, by far, the most popular form of media consuming our preteens' time. From personal Web spaces to online games to instant messaging, even students in the fourth, fifth, and sixth grades spend hours a day online.

Another interesting aspect of the current preteen generation is that while some are star-struck by celebrity, they generally don't seem to have role models—they're content to be their own persons. In fact, they're very wary about allowing others to influence the way they dress, what music they listen to, or what they should or should not believe. This can actually be a good thing, because once preteens decide to believe something, they believe with a passion. What better incentive do we need to continually find new and inventive ways to point them to Jesus?

I saw this for myself in our sixth-grade ministry this past year. Amy (name changed) was only 11 years old when she started off the year asking hard questions: How do we know that Jesus is really God's Son? How do I know God really loves me? How can I make this faith my own and not just something my parents have taught me all my life? Amy struggled with these questions for over six months until she recently chose to follow Christ. During an interview with her, she said that she finally just *gave up* on God. She'd been going through the motions (this is a sixth-grader talking!), thinking that God didn't care about her and that she should just ignore it all. However, through her interactions with her discipleship leader and other caring believers interested in reaching kids her age, Amy felt the pull of the Holy Spirit. She said it drew her so strongly to the gospel that her heart had no choice but to cave in to the claims of Christ. Now this young lady is truly committed to telling others about Jesus and making the passion of her life known—a genuine relationship with God. Once preteens make a decision and believe something, some have a boldness that even their parents don't have in proclaiming how they feel and what they believe. Amy is living proof of that!

So what are the trends in preteen ministry today, and where is the ministry to this age group headed?

- *Churches recognize and respond to the unique needs of preteens.* At Perimeter Church, we've found that separating our sixth-grade ministry from the others best meets their needs. To give them their own space, sixth-graders meet each Sunday in their own "neighborhood" of KIDSTown, a themed environment we've created just for kids. Their fellowship time begins in a game room with pool tables, ping-pong, air hockey, foosball, and a cool cafe where snacks are served periodically. On the first and third Sundays of each month, sixth-graders gather in the "Uptown Auditorium" for a large-group teaching time designed specifically for preteens. Lessons incorporate PowerPoint, fun videos, drama, games, and dynamic youth-oriented teaching to reach our sixth-graders for Christ. To accommodate our emphasis on discipleship, accountability, and the building of relationships, kids are divided into small groups of six to seven students on the second and fourth Sundays. An adult leader facilitates each group and serves as guide and mentor to help kids build a strong knowledge of God and his Word.

  And because our church considers fourth- and fifth-grade students to be preteens as well, we're committed to a vital, relative ministry that speaks just to them in their walk with God. Intentional discipleship is the foundation of our ministry, and that begins even with this age group. We model their time together after that of their sixth-grade friends—and as with the sixth-graders, discipling and relationship-building (with each other and with God) are the focus.

150   CHILDREN'S MINISTRY IN THE 21ST CENTURY

- ***Traditional Sunday school structures transform.*** Churches answer the need for consistent life-on-life discipleship with preteens. Traditional Sunday school slowly gives way to small groups led by dedicated adults who fully invest in the lives of those preteen students within their groups. While grade-specific curriculum is used to help kids grow in their understanding of God, the key to these discipleship groups is the building of relationships. Churches who've adopted this model of teaching now reap a great harvest—and the cool thing is, recruiting is no longer a major issue! At our church, adults not only respond positively to this new ministry—they actually *ask* to lead discipleship groups for these kids. Building relationships through discipleship draws not only preteens but lay leaders as well.

- ***Children's ministry focuses on authenticity, not "churchianity."*** Today's generation of preteens has an aversion to anything legalistic or "churchy." Understanding this is key in ministering to preteens. As pastor to fourth- through sixth-graders, I seek to model transparency and *realness* with the students—and I ask that our preteen discipleship leaders and lay volunteers do the same. Of course, we must use wise judgment regarding what we share with our preteen students, but today's kids can sense a fake a mile away. The more one *pretends* to "have it all together" or come across as *religious* rather than scripturally spiritual, the less fruit that person will likely see while ministering to preteens. Kids respond to honesty about our shortcomings and sins. And this gives us the opportunity to share about how God is working in and through us in *spite* of our sins. Don't be reserved—specifically *name* sins that are appropriate to talk about with preteen students. As kids sense your authenticity, they'll have an even greater hunger to know a God who'll love them unconditionally. After all, Psalm 51:6 says, "Surely you desire truth from the inner parts; you teach me wisdom in the inmost place" (New International Version).

While there really is no set rule or pattern for success in reaching today's preteens, one thing is certain: We'll lose them if we don't meet them where they are. And understanding this truth is actually an exciting, liberating thing—replace certain tired conventions and stale traditions with vibrant, energetic models of teaching and reaching kids. Gather your lay leaders, volunteers, and even parents for fun brainstorming sessions ushering your children's ministry into the 21st century! And then thank God for the harvest.

RESOURCES FOR FURTHER STUDY

(I recommend these books if you want to know more about trends in preteen ministry and the church in general.)

Barna, George, *Transforming Children Into Spiritual Champions*. Ventura, CA: Regal Books, 2003.

Peterson, Eugene, *The Message: The Bible in Contemporary Language*. Colorado Springs, CO: NavPress, 2002. (This is an incredible Bible to use with preteens!)

Pope, Randy, *The Intentional Church*. Chicago, IL: Moody Publishers, 2006.

Scazzero, Peter, *The Emotionally Healthy Church*. Grand Rapids, MI: Zondervan, 2003.

Try This

BY BECKI MANNI

Activity 1

PRETEEN ACTIVITIES

Kids this age thrive on the experiential. They want to be "in the moment," they're very creative, and they can now cognitively understand many of the complexities and abstract aspects of how God interacts with his people.

I WAS THERE

Kids will relive the Passover or Last Supper instead of only hearing or reading about them. Contact a local messianic Jewish congregation who would be willing to come in and do a Seder or the Passover meal for your group. If this isn't an option, research Seders online. (Try this Web site: http://www.jewfaq.org/seder.htm.) To be true to the Last Supper, recreate it from a Christian's perspective, and emphasize that Jesus is the central focus. If recreating the original Passover, emphasize how the elements point prophetically to the coming of Christ so many years later. Be careful of making this too childish. Kids this age want to feel they're old enough to understand the complexities and foretelling of the original event.

Create an atmosphere for them that's reminiscent of the original. If re-enacting the Passover, read through Exodus 13 to get ideas. Assign preteens to "families," and have them stand around the tables to eat hurriedly. Use a fog machine to create the atmosphere of the Lord passing over. Use your sound system to generate the sounds of soldiers and the grieving Egyptians outside the "house." Use washable poster paints to spread the blood of the lamb over the doorposts. Allow them to experience the bitter herbs, the taste of roasted lamb, and the bread without yeast. Each food eaten for Passover has deep meaning and allusion. Explain this as you proceed with the meal.

If re-enacting the Last Supper, read Luke 22 for ideas. Lay your tables on the floor with the legs folded and surround them with pillows. Give preteens each a disciple's name and ask them to play the role of that disciple sitting where that man did. Adult leaders may play the role of Jesus, as this is the person who moves through the elements of the service with the kids. Begin with the foot washing, substituting hand washing for those who may be uncomfortable removing their shoes. If you have more than 13 kids in your group, break them into individual tables. Set the tables with the items served at the Last Supper, substituting watered-down grape juice for the wine yet staying as true to the biblical rendition as possible. Remind kids why this is a solemn occasion, and create an atmosphere in the room that reinforces this. You may even choose to carry the re-enactment as far as having them leave the room to go "out to the garden" to close in prayer.

After your re-enactment, discuss:

For the Passover:

- **What do you think the Passover has to do with your lives today?**
- **What's the meaning of spreading the blood over the doorframes during the Passover?**
- **How could you celebrate your own "present day" Passover each year?**

For the Last Supper:

- **How would you have felt if you were there that night?**
- **What do you think Jesus meant when he said the wine and the bread were his body and blood?**
- **Why do you think Jesus washed each person's feet?**
- **How would this event have been different had Jesus come this year?**

Activity 2

BUILD YOUR OWN TABERNACLE

This can be an ongoing project over several weeks or compressed into a one-week event, depending on the depth with which you choose to explore it. Just as Moses did, assign kids roles to play based on their gifts and talents. The key is to get everyone involved on a personal level and to "live" the adventure. Some may be good at drawing, some at sewing, and some at sculpting, and some may thrive on writing psalms of praise for the dedication of the tabernacle to God. By giving kids responsibility, you create buy-in, and they will "own" the project. You may even choose to appoint Levites as priests and fashion the priestly garments.

Optional lessons may include rebuilding the ark or Solomon's Temple. Whatever you choose to study, the key is to put the preteens into the event as realistically as possible and then to explore their feelings, reactions, and applications of the experience to their own lives.

Afterward, discuss:

- **What would it have been like to create the Temple of God? How would being involved have affected your relationship with God?**
- **How did building this temple affect your relationship with God?**
- **Why do you think Moses had so many people involved in building the Temple?**
- **How did it feel to play an important role in building something together for God?**
- **Is there something in our lives that we as a group can work on together for God?**

Activity 3

THE LAST WEEK OF JESUS' LIFE

Taking each of the events from the arrest of Jesus in the garden to the day of resurrection, assign roles based on the elements of the story. These are not roles to be played out in front of the group but roles to immerse themselves in as deeply as possible. The goal here is to get kids to "walk in that person's shoes"—to feel what those people felt and then to dissect how that would have changed their own lives had they truly lived it. You may choose to have them "read their lines" directly from the Bible or to rewrite their lines based on how they live today.

Challenge them to analyze how it would have felt to be Simon the Cyrene and to carry Jesus' cross by having them carry a heavy piece of wood across their backs. Challenge them to examine how they would have acted had they been in Pilate's shoes by having a crowd of kids demanding them to do something scary. Challenge them to step into the moment by "flogging" an old log or pounding a piece of uncooked meat. Challenge them to explore the life of the character they have been assigned. What was it like to be a girl in those events, or a priest, thief, or soldier?

Don't allow them to settle for the typical "Sunday school" answers but to really dig deep and apply the lessons to their own lives by keeping the focus on the reality and the feelings of living the event. It is OK at this age to let them feel disgust, fear, anger or any of the negative feelings we tend to shy away from with younger children. Kids this age know what it is to feel these feelings, and it drives the point home even deeper to know Jesus and those in the Bible were real people with real feelings.

Afterward, discuss:
- **What was it like to walk in that person's shoes and have to make the decisions he or she did?**
- **How would this series of events have been different if Jesus had been born in the 20th century?**
- **After living this character's life experience, how did your view of Jesus change? How did your view of the event change?**

Activity 4

TEACHING JESUS' PARABLES

Rather than having these lessons taught by the leader, assign the parables to small groups of kids, and challenge them to teach the parable to their peers as creatively as possible. Tell them they'll also have to lead the discussion afterward and that the focus will be on applying the lesson to real life in the 21st century. They may use video, a PowerPoint presentation, re-enactment, or any number of methods to immerse the class in the parable. They'll provide props, questions, and snacks, or whatever necessary to get the group to live it out. They're responsible to teach as Jesus taught. This builds "buy-in" and results in real life change.

By making the kids responsible for teaching their peers, they're challenged to think the point through in depth. This takes them beyond the story of mustard seeds, lost sheep, or prodigal sons. They have to research, investigate, and apply the lesson to present-day life. This gives them insight and practical solutions to dealing with the challenges they face of peer pressure, isolation, self-esteem, and bullies, or even deciding for themselves what faith in Jesus means. Challenge them to see Jesus as someone who didn't fit the norm, someone who challenged social influences. These are all common trials to kids in middle school.

Afterward, discuss:

- **What did it mean to you to "teach as Jesus taught"?**
- **How did this assignment change the way you think about Jesus? your life? your relationship with Jesus?**
- **How has this lesson changed how you will approach your life in the future?**

Activity 5

PIZZA PROVISION

Help preteens understand the problem of hunger in our world. Order a pizza for your preteens or make one yourself. Set out a pizza cutter, plates, plastic knives, and cups of water. Tell kids that your class represents all the 6 billion people in the world, but that not all people enjoy the same provisions.

Divide kids into two groups: one group of about a fifth of your total group, and everyone else in the second group. For example, if you have 15 kids, one group would be three and the other would be 12. Cut the pizza into eight slices, and give one slice to the largest group and the remainder to the smaller group. Provide water to drink, and have kids share the pizza in their groups. Then discuss:

- **How did you feel about the piece of pizza you ate?**
- **Do you think the portion you received was fair? Why or why not?**

Explain to preteens that approximately 20 percent of the wealthiest people in the world consume about 85 percent of the world's food and services. In fact, the poorest 20 percent of the world's population get only about one percent of the food and services! Then spend some time brainstorming with your preteens what your class can do, individually and as a group, to help the hungry in the world. You might want to visit sites such as www.worldvision.org. (And be sure to have some extra pizza saved for the group that didn't get much!)

Activity 6

FRIENDSHIP CARDS FROM JESUS

Talk to preteens about how friends say encouraging and supporting words when they're working together toward a goal; they celebrate the joys of their triumphs and hold on to each other when things are falling to pieces.

Write these verses on a chalkboard or a piece of butcher paper: John 3:16-17; 4:13-14; 10:9-10; 10:14-15; 11:25-27; 15:9-17; 20:29; 21:15-17. Give each preteen two or three sheets of paper, a marker, and a Bible. Have preteens choose two or three of these verses and use their papers and markers to design "Friendship Cards From Jesus" based on the meaning of the passages. They should write the cards as if Jesus were writing them.

For example, if they choose John 10:14-15, they might design cards with sheep on the front and a message on the inside that says: "I would lay down my life for you. In fact, I did! You are that important to me. I love you! Your best friend, Jesus."

After preteens have created their cards, have them form trios to share the messages in their cards. Afterward, discuss:

- **Why is it important to see Jesus as a friend?**
- **How do these passages make you feel?**
- **How can we be good friends to one another and share Jesus' love with our friends?**

Encourage preteens to decide on one person they know whom they'd like to give their friendship cards to as a sign of friendship and a reminder of Jesus' love.

Activity 7

FINDING OUR WAY

There are many voices calling out to preteens, telling them which way to go. Do this fun activity to help them experience how helpful good guidance can be. Designate starting and ending points for an obstacle course, and tell preteens where they are. (The ending point should be a doorway, if possible.) Form two groups and have each preteen put on a blindfold. Then arrange chairs and other furniture to create obstacles. Make sure kids will have to walk around lots of objects as if in a life-size maze. Go to the first group, and turn some of the kids to disorient them.

Tell kids it's their job to carefully get from the starting point to the ending point. Tell them you'll time them to see how long it takes for everyone to complete the course. Don't allow any talking or moving of obstacles. Have the first group go through the obstacle course and keep their blindfolds on until the second group has completed the course.

When the second group goes through the course, call out directions to this group. After both groups have completed the course, have kids take off their blindfolds and form a circle. Tell them how long it took for each group to complete the course. Afterward, discuss:

- **How did you feel trying to get through this course?**
- **How is that like the way you feel as you work your way through the obstacles of life?**
- **Read John 14:26. How does Jesus promise to help us and guide us?**
- **How can we learn to listen to God's guidance for our lives?**

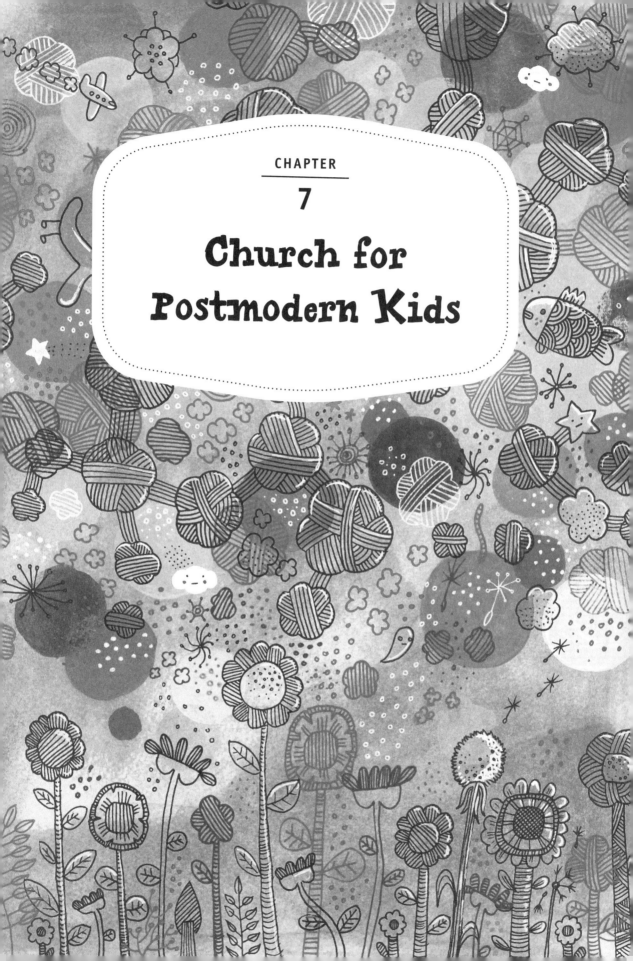

CHAPTER

7

Church for Postmodern Kids

THE EMERGENT CHURCH

BY SHARYN SPRADLIN

In the last half of the 20th century, the spiritual design of the Western world experienced a major renovation—a renovation in which commitment to the traditional structures of the modern-era church has steadily declined, while at the same time a yearning for the spiritual climbed to the forefront of the cultural dialogue. Unmarked by any one historical event, this renovation has been based on vast changes in our institutions, social structures, and the globalization of culture. The way we view the world has radically changed, causing a shift in how we think, learn, and communicate.

You might be saying, "OK, so what does this have to do with children's ministry? What does this postmodern stuff have to do with me?"

Postmodernism has *everything* to do with you and your genuine interest in ministering to kids today. The kids sitting in your classrooms didn't experience the modern age you may have grown up in. They're postmodern.

MODERN TIMES

Postmodern literally means "after modern." So what's *modern*? It's not the adjective, meaning the latest and most up-to-date. Modernism refers to a philosophical movement.

Roughly beginning in the 1700s, the ideas of modernism gained popularity—people began to believe that the power of objective knowledge, reason, and science would lead to the perfect society and save the world. That has carried through until now. In the 20th century, nearly every part of our Western values and beliefs were dominated by the belief that information would bring transformation.

So even the church adopted the *teaching* model for spiritual formation. Our facilities were designed for the giving and receiving of instruction—evidenced by the classroom-like environment. Our organizational structures were patterned after the hierarchy of our governments and universities. And faith communicated through the creative arts, thought to be irrelevant and distracting, was stripped from the church in many cases.

It's true—the modern age has provided many things that have greatly helped humanity, such as broadcast communication and modern medical treatments. However, it has also suppressed our humanity. By only considering what's called "reason," "science," and "objective knowledge," the mysteries of life and the supernatural are extinguished in our minds. This value system is turned on its head for the postmodernist. Objectivity, analysis, and control are thought to be archaic, and more value is given to the mystery and wonder of our world.

THINGS AREN'T WHAT THEY SEEM

So, what exactly is postmodernism? How do we define it?

How very modernistic of you to ask!

The very question itself asks for boundaries—describing what it is or isn't. Postmodernism resists being identified by distinct characteristics or descriptive analogies. Many postmodernists believe that all things are relative, dependent on an individual's perspective and circumstance. Things aren't necessarily what they seem because there's no center and no guiding principles. Those who've grown up with modernistic assumptions (such as knowledge is progressive, certain, and objective) will receive strong reaction from the postmodernist when it comes to religious institutions and dogma.

Although the church began as a movement, it has gradually mutated into a culture-driven institution shaped by modernist values. It operates with the efficiency of the industrial age, defining success in terms of attendance, budgets, buildings, and programs. Churches have claimed knowledge as their own and market this knowledge and its transforming power to reach potential consumers.

It would be impossible to overstate the impact of postmodernism on the institutional church that has thrived in this modernist form. The institution of modernism defies everything the postmodern pilgrim on a spiritual journey believes.

The Christian church of the Western world is at a defining moment in its history. Call it a shakedown, shift, or transition. Things are changing from the orderly, predictable, and dependable modern way to the postmodern way. We are well into the transition, and there's no way to tell what'll emerge in the future.

Nervous?

This could be more than a little unsettling. After all, if there's no framework to guide one's spiritual direction, where will we end up? But there's also great opportunity here: Although the postmodern era can be characterized by its lack of absolutes and traditional values, the postmodern individual is often far more open to spirituality than previous generations.

IMAGINE A CHURCH FOR THE POSTMODERN

Imagine a church that's become more flexible and organic, changing to engage the culture around it. Imagine the opportunity to redesign how the church carries out its mission. Imagine re-examining the plan laid out in Scripture to become an authentic community doing life together.

Last year at Children's Ministry Magazine Live workshops, we prepared a learning experience that focused on rebuilding the church. We gave each small group a sheet of paper to represent the church. Members of the group wrote their names in large letters on the papers, showing that they were a part of the community. They then shared a time they experienced conflict or hurt with another member of the church. As people shared, they tore the paper to represent the brokenness they felt and that the church experienced. After everyone shared, the conversation turned to God's ability to build something new through our brokenness. We then had groups piece their papers back together while discussing how they'd experienced God's healing in their lives. At no time were the groups instructed to put the pieces back into the original form (as an 8 ½x11-inch sheet). There were no restrictions, no boundaries—only the guidelines that they be put back together.

What a beautiful example of the church. A whole new way of doing church can develop. New types of communities need to be envisioned and created to be the message in this new era. Simply adapting existing church structures won't enable new and appropriate expressions of the kingdom to arise for new generations.

Remember the torn paper groups? Less than 5 percent of the groups formed their torn pieces into something other than 8 ½x11-inch sheets of paper. Why? Huge assumptions clutter our minds, blocking anything new that God might want to create. So much of what we've come to know as church has been shaped by Christendom rather than by Scripture.

So for a moment, imagine there are no models to follow, no curriculum to purchase, no regimented program, not even a movement to speak of. Imagine there's only a global conversation—a conversation about a new kind of church.

WHAT'S EMERGING

There's a new breed of churches emerging. Some call them the "new church," others refer to them as the "emergent church." They aren't well-organized; there's no common denominational affiliation. Many have emerged as a reaction to the modern Western church, but they by no means discard the heart of the Christian church.

The emergent church is mission-focused. Seeing itself as a part of a larger expression of God's presence, the emergent church believes Jesus intended us to interact with the culture around us. The emergent church faces the needs of the world, ready to practice its faith to reach the needs of others. Reaching the postmodern requires authentic relationships where the love of Christ is demonstrated before a spiritual seeker ever walks through the door of a church.

The emergent church is about relationships. The gospel is all about the formation of community, the responsibility we as followers of Jesus have to each other and to those outside the faith. As we draw closer to God, we draw closer to one another. And as we draw closer to each other, we come to understand God more closely as he works through his community of believers.

The emergent church is about participation and experience. Efforts toward designing contemporary worship have received much attention in the last decade or more. Postmodern worship is not simply a matter of style, but a focus on creating an environment in which worshippers don't just hear about the power of God, they experience it.

The emergent church is image-rich. Tremendous change has occurred in communication and popular media. Our world relays information visually through images that are absorbed at a glance and that often transcend language barriers. Images have become the language of postmodernism. Why? Images connect in a way that words can't. Seen through each individual's eyes, they tantalize emotions and eventually invade the heart because they cause a reaction. This visual experience is more than just an old overhead projector. It's more about creatively communicating a message that a postmodern connects with through new visual concepts and methods.

Images are hardly new to the church. Centuries ago, the world looked to the church for images to communicate and interpret the Word. Some of the greatest artists in the world focused on the Gospels as their primary topic of expression. Sculptures, paintings, and stained glass told the story of our Savior to a mostly illiterate culture. The emergent church is again discovering this rich method of communication.

EMBRACE THE OPPORTUNITIES

This new way of envisioning church goes beyond merely surviving the cultural changes and challenges of the postmodern era. It embraces the change as opportunity. More than any other time or generation this century, people are open to the spiritual. They're not interested in organized religion, but they are interested in Jesus.

As a leader of children, you have the opportunity to contextualize the message of Jesus and the truth of the Scriptures for the culture they've grown up in. Don't just teach from the front of a classroom; develop authentic relationships with them. Instead of simply lecturing, enable children to participate in, experience, and discover the truths of Scripture. Take advantage of opportunities to touch your children through images and artistic expression. Committing to change takes determination, great faith, intentionality, and a clear understanding that there are no quick fixes. But your commitment will draw children into a deep, rich relationship with Jesus!

Try This

BY VICKI L.O. WITTE

Activity 1

PRAYING WITH PICTURES

Help kids learn about intercessory prayer with this media activity. Prepare a slide show, including images of people and things kids can pray about. This could either be very broad or quite specific. For example, for a missions emphasis you might include maps of a particular region, native people who live there, missionaries your church supports there, water sources, crops, and so on. Or you might wish to be broader in scope, showing things like hungry children, a modern hospital, soldiers, teachers, or firefighters all in the same slide show. The scope and variety are up to you.

Before starting the slide show, say: **We can make a big difference when we pray for others, but sometimes it's hard to know where to begin! Most of us pray for our families or our friends, but did you know you can have an impact on people you don't even know? We can do that right now—watch this.**

Show the slide show at a normal speed first, and invite the children to simply take it all in. Then tell kids you'll repeat the slide show, stopping on certain images for a moment. When you pause on an image, kids can offer sentence prayers aloud for the person or object they see on the slide. For instance, if you show a picture of a child, kids can pray that that child will know God or will have enough to eat. Or if you stop on a farm field, kids can pray that the farmer will harvest lots of crops this year.

Repeat the slide show, but only pause on about four photos (it's more important that kids engage thoughtfully in a few slides than impatiently in many). Be sure to remind children that if they're uncomfortable praying aloud, that's OK; God hears the prayers of our hearts, too.

When you've gone through all the slides and children are finished praying, close the prayer time by saying something like this: **Lord, hear our prayers. In Jesus' name, amen.** Then ask:

- **How would it make you feel to know people were praying for you?**
- **Why is it important to pray even for people we don't know?**
- **How can we remind ourselves to pray for others?**

Activity 2

SENIORS AND JUNIORS

Help your church practice community with this fun partnering activity.

Pair up each child in your class or children's ministry with an older person in the church. Take individual photos of the kids and the adults, and label the photos by name. Give each child the picture of his or her adult partner, and give each adult the picture of his or her child partner. Encourage partners to share prayer requests and commit to pray for each other regularly.

Arrange for the pairs to meet together about quarterly to nurture their relationships. For example, you might kick off the program with a pizza party for everyone. At Christmastime, arrange for a party with an inexpensive gift exchange between partners. St. Patrick's Day or Easter might offer another occasion for a party. And celebrate the end of the school year with a summer barbecue! Continue the partnerships for at least a year. At that time evaluate whether to continue as is, to switch partners, or to begin again with a different age group of children or a different group of adults.

At the end of the year, gather all partners together to share their experiences as a large group. Have partners read Proverbs 20:29 together, then ask:

- **What was the best part about having a partner who's older/younger?**
- **What did you learn from your partner? What were you able to teach your partner?**
- **How can the "strength" of the young bring glory to God? What about the "gray hair of experience"?**

Activity 3

PRAYERFUL READING

Teach children to soak in Scripture with this quiet reading activity. Explain that it might be different from anything they've done before, and they might feel kind of strange doing it at first, but you'd like them to try something new.

Let the children get comfortable around the room, spaced far enough apart that they can't touch each other. You may want to dim the lights for this activity. Invite kids to relax and listen to your voice.

Tell kids that you will read a few verses of Scripture. They should listen while you read and notice if any particular word or phrase jumps out at them. You'll read the passage through three times, so they should simply listen to your voice. Be sure to choose a short passage—just a few lines if your children are very young!

Read the Bible verse(s) slowly and clearly. Then repeat two more times. Tell the children to silently repeat to themselves whatever word or phrase stuck out to them during the reading, thinking about whatever comes to their minds.

After a few moments, ask the children to pray silently about whatever thoughts came to their minds. Give them time to do this.

For example, you might read Psalm 103:2-4 to children several times:

"Let all that I am praise the Lord;
   may I never forget the good things he does for me.
He forgives all my sins
   and heals all my diseases.
He redeems me from death
   and crowns me with love and tender mercies."

The phrase "tender mercies" may stand out to kids, and they can think quietly about what this means to them. Then they can pray and thank God for his mercy toward them. (Depending on the age of your kids, you may need to help them understand some words.)

After the prayer time, call the children together. Invite the children to share the words or phrases that jumped out at them from the Bible reading. Don't insist that anyone share, but do give children the opportunity.

When they're finished sharing, discuss these questions:
• **What was different about listening to the Bible this way?**
• **How can reading the Bible slowly like this help you to pray?**

Activity 4

ARTFUL PRAYER

Teach children to express their prayers creatively with this art activity.

Let each child choose a sheet of drawing paper or construction paper and an assortment of crayons. Explain that you'll all spread around the room so that everyone has space to think and to draw. Emphasize that this will be quiet time, so tell the children to get comfortable and relax.

Pray aloud, asking God to hear each child, then encourage kids to pray silently. Let kids know they can simply tell God how much they love him. They can also give thanks to him, or they can pray for someone who needs help. Remind them that they can simply spend time with God without saying anything at all. After about two minutes, have kids draw or color whatever comes to their minds. These pictures might be nothing more than colors or abstract designs, or they might be detailed pictures of things they spoke to God about. Give the children several minutes of silence to complete this activity.

When the coloring time is up, call the children back together. Explain that no one should comment on anyone else's pictures, since these are between each child and God. Do invite the children to share their pictures if they wish to, and display them if possible.

After the activity, discuss these questions:

- **Was it hard to concentrate for two whole minutes? What sorts of things can help us stay focused on God as we pray?**
- **What was it like to express yourself by drawing after your prayer?**

Activity 5

EXPERIENTIAL PRAYER STATIONS

Help children learn different types of prayer by experiencing each at prayer stations.

Before class, set up four prayer stations around your room. The stations will correspond to the four parts of the ACTS prayer model: Adoration, Confession, Thanksgiving, and Supplication.

Say: **God doesn't keep track of the types of prayers we pray. In fact, one of the best parts about having a friendship with Jesus is that we can talk to him about anything on our minds, anytime we want. But understanding types of prayers can help us remember to thank God or to tell him how much we love him. It can remind us to tell him we're sorry for things we've done or to pray for other people. Let's experience those types of prayers as we go through different prayer stations.**

Let the children move through these stations at their own pace, in any order. This may happen over the course of several weeks as you teach about prayer. The youth and adults of your church might benefit from the prayer stations as well. If you have a younger group, talk with the children about what each word means before they go through the stations.

Adoration

At the Adoration Station, set out a variety of artificial flowers and ribbons. Also, prop up a card that says: "When we adore someone, we love everything about that person. We want to give that person beautiful things, like flowers. Make a bouquet for God, and tell him one thing you love about him for each flower in the bouquet." (Read cards at the stations aloud for younger kids.)

Confession

At the Confession Station, set out an Etch A Sketch or similar "erasable" toy. Prop up a card that says: "When we see how great God is, we see the sins in our own life. Tell God about the sins you are sorry for, and make some kind of mark or design on the Etch A Sketch. If you ask God to forgive you, he will erase your sins. Now erase the mark you made!"

Thanksgiving

At the Thanksgiving Station, set out construction paper and colored markers. Prop up a card that says: "There are some things we thank God for all the time. But try to think of five things you've never thanked God for before. Write them down as a thank-you card to God, and thank him for them now."

Supplication

At the Supplication Station, set out a variety of adhesive bandages and a sign or poster that says "Supplication." Stick one bandage on the sign. Set out a card that says: "Supplication means praying that God will help other people. Who do you know that needs help? Pray for those people now. Write each person's name on the white part of a bandage, then stick that bandage on the 'Supplication' poster."

After the children have experienced all the prayer stations, ask:

- **If Jesus were sitting next to you on the school bus or on your couch at home, what would you probably talk to him about?**
- **Which type of prayer do you sometimes forget to pray? What can you do to remember to include this in your prayer time?**
- **Which type of prayer is most comfortable for you to pray? Why do you think that is?**

Activity 6

FAITH SHARING

Help your church experience community and value kids' faith journeys with this worship activity.

At some point during your worship service each week, incorporate a time of faith sharing. During this time, a child will share a story from his or her life about how he or she has seen Jesus at work. It could be a story from home or school, or a story that is somehow related to the church family.

Let the child share in his or her own words what it meant to see Jesus working in that way. Sometimes you may want to invite an entire family to share about a particular experience, such as a family mission trip or service project—just be sure to remind them that the children get to speak as much as the adults!

If you want to help prepare the children ahead of time, ask them to think about these questions:

- **What happened?**
- **How did you see Jesus in that story?**
- **How did that make you feel?** or **What did that mean to you?** or **What did you learn from that?**

After several weeks of hearing from the children in your church, ask some of the children who have shared what that experience of sharing was like for them. Ask the other children what it was like for them to listen to other children's stories.

Activity 7

KIDS' WORSHIP

Get your kids involved in the experience of worship, and get them thinking about why we worship at church.

Let the kids take over the worship planning for a week—or more! You may be pleasantly surprised by the results. Three rules: everyone must be involved in the planning; everyone must be involved in the implementation; and you are the facilitator only—you will coach, guide, and encourage, but the kids must do the work.

Guide your children's class or children's ministry in planning an entire worship service. You may want to start gently by providing them with the basic structure your church uses for the order of worship and letting the kids fill in the specifics: they can choose the songs and readings, write the prayers, and suggest a passage or topic for the sermon. Then let the kids decide who will lead the songs, readings, and prayers; greet worshippers; collect the offering; and so on.

If you're feeling more daring, let the kids start from scratch. Encourage them to brainstorm about what they would like to do in church, understanding that it must ultimately bring glory to God. Help them evaluate and organize their ideas and put them in a form your congregation could use. Again, the kids must decide who will lead each activity.

After the child-led service, ask the kids:
- **What was it like to plan this worship service? Why?**
- **What was it like to lead this worship service? Why?**
- **What did you learn about why we worship God?**

Activity 8

SECRET WORSHIP

Give your kids a taste of both ancient and international worship with this creative worship experience.

Darken your meeting room, covering the windows if possible. Instead of using ordinary lights, drape a few strings of white or clear Christmas lights around the room. (You could also use candles, but with children of any age, Christmas lights are infinitely safer!) Push the chairs and tables to the edges of the room, and place rugs and pillows on the floor instead.

Explain that in the early days of Christianity, it was dangerous in some places for Christians to meet together to worship. They had to hide out in secret in order to worship Jesus, and if they were caught they would be severely punished or even killed. Today that's still true in some countries. But that doesn't stop people who love Jesus from worshipping him!

Point out the darkened windows and the special lights, and explain that today you're going to worship like those people who have to worship in secret. Encourage kids to huddle together while you sing their favorite songs together. Let them imagine what it must be like to love Jesus enough to risk their lives to worship him. Have children share their prayer requests and pray for each other in the darkened room, too. Remind them that because they're worshipping in secret, they'll need to keep their voices down.

At the end of your worship time, read Hebrews 13:3 to the children. Then ask these questions:

- **What was it like to worship this way? Why?**
- **If you were told that you weren't allowed to worship God, what do you think you'd do?**
- **How did this experience help you appreciate your own freedom to worship?**
- **How can you remember to pray for those who aren't free to worship?**

Close your time together by praying for those Christians around the world who are persecuted for their faith in Jesus.

To take this experience one step further, teach children about specific countries where Christians aren't allowed to worship freely. Visit www.bibleleague.org/persecuted to learn about the persecuted church. Lead children in praying specifically for people in these countries. You could also do this experience on the International Day of Prayer for the Persecuted Church in November. Visit www.persecutedchurch.org for more information.

Activity 9

OUTDOOR CHURCH

Help children gain a new perspective of their surroundings and their relationship with God with this creative worship experience.

Take your children's class outdoors for worship one day. You might want to recruit a few extra adult volunteers to help you keep kids safe, corralled, and attentive.

Begin with a quiet walk. Invite the children to observe their surroundings as you walk—whether you are in a rural, suburban, or urban area. After a few minutes, have the children sit down and close their eyes. Invite them to simply be still and listen to all the sounds around them. After a few minutes, invite kids to share what they saw and heard.

Next, ask each child to choose one object that best represents his or her relationship with God at this particular time. For example, one child might choose a dandelion because of how it continues to grow, even under bad conditions. Another child might choose a dead stick, because he or she is feeling distant from God. Give the children a few minutes to choose their objects, and then take a few minutes to let them share why they chose what they did.

As you guide the children back to your regular meeting place, lead them in praise to God for all they see and hear around them. When you've returned to your room, ask children these questions:

- **What did you think about worshipping outdoors this way?**
- **How is outdoor worship different from worshipping in a building? How is it the same?**

Activity 10

OFF-SITE WORSHIP

Give children opportunities for outreach and imaginative thinking with these creative worship ideas.

If grown-up church gets to meet in coffee shops and bookstores, turnabout for children is fair play, right? You'll want to recruit some extra helpers to join you on these off-site excursions.

If "big church" is meeting in a local bookstore, why not simply take the children to the children's section? What better place to share the great stories of faith! Explain that the Bible is the best story of all, especially because it's true. If there are kids in the bookstore that aren't from your group, invite them to join your kids as you tell the greatest story ever told.

Another great place to worship with kids, assuming you have plenty of help for supervision, is the local park or playground. Use the wide-open spaces and even the playground equipment to act out the Bible stories with the kids. You can make a joyful noise to the Lord without disturbing other classes! And invite the children to simply revel in God's creativity and goodness.

After enjoying an off-site worship experience, discuss these questions with the children:

• **What was it like to worship in that place? Why?**
• **Where are some other places you'd like to worship?**
• **What types of places help you feel closest to Jesus?**

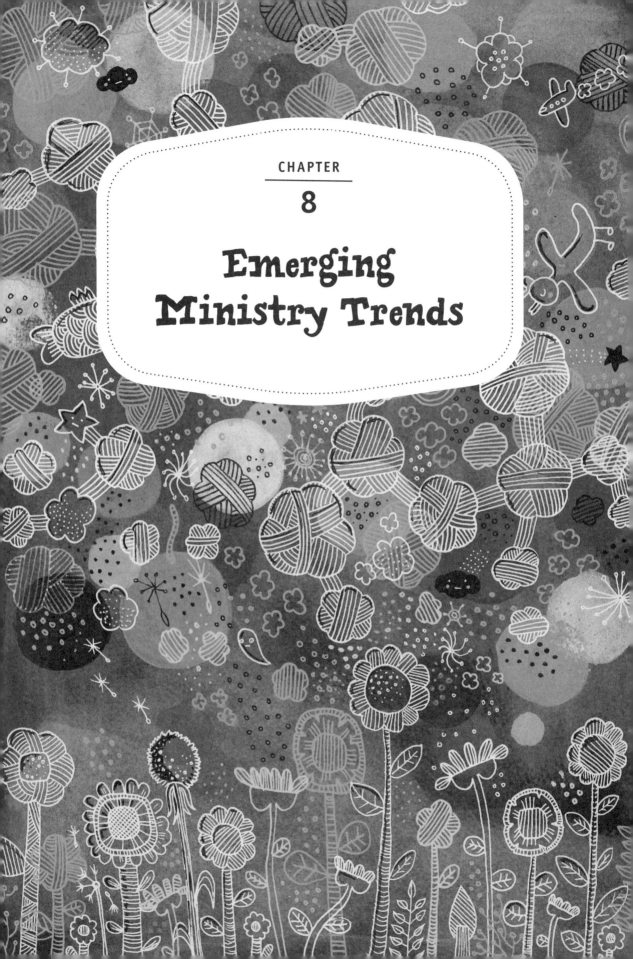

CHAPTER

8

Emerging Ministry Trends

A CHANGE IN THE WEATHER

BY JIM WIDEMAN

To me, one of the most intriguing professions in the world is that of a meteorologist. Forecasting the weather is a really tough job—especially if you live where I do in the southern Midwest. You've probably heard the saying: "If you don't like the weather, stick around for another 15 minutes. It'll change!" Well, that's a lot like today's culture. Don't get too used to any particular way of doing things—if you wait just a little bit, it'll probably change. And that's why, like a meteorologist, children's ministry leaders need to forecast.

A key trend emerging in children's ministry is that churches are realizing the need to rethink what "they've always done" to reach kids they hadn't reached in the past. At Church On The Move, we're forecasting and planning—not for the children's ministry we have now, but for the one we want to have even 15 years down the road. We've spent a lot of time reinventing ourselves so we'll captivate today's preschool child when that same child is in upper-elementary grades.

The biggest problem I see with so many churches is that they can't look ahead for looking behind. I believe it's time for churches to take Paul's advice in Philippians 3:13-14: "No, dear brothers and sisters, I have not achieved it, but I focus on this one thing: Forgetting the past and looking forward to what lies ahead, I press on to reach the end of the race and receive the heavenly prize for which God, through Christ Jesus, is calling us." Did you hear what he said? Forget the past and look forward to what's ahead. We need to quit looking at the way we've always done things and consider instead what'll launch us into current and future cultures. Let's concentrate on what tomorrow's church will look like and effectively train kids now so they can take their place in that church.

To put it simply, we need to wake up and smell the millennium! Jesus himself set this example by coming into our world to reach us right where we were—right on our level. Like Jesus, we must be willing to go into the world of today's child. The way I see it, it's been almost 40 years since I was a kid—the world has changed since then, and so should my teaching methods.

IDENTIFY NEEDS AND FORECAST

1. **Read everything you can about upcoming trends.** I want to commend you for purchasing this book, but don't let your quest end here. Subscribe to Children's Ministry Magazine and other publications that explore the future of kids on a regular basis. Do an Internet search for "children's ministry" and "educational trends" to learn what's new, and be a constant student of what's ahead.

2. **Immerse yourself in studying "kid culture."** Not just church kid culture, but know the world that today's kids are a part of—its music, its values, its definitions and wrappings. I've been a student of kid culture for over 30 years, and this study has helped me keep my children's ministry in a state of constant change. I spend more time studying what media giants are doing to capture kids than what the traditional church continues to do. The only churches I study are the ones who are studying culture.

3. **Implement what you learn.** I've been asking this for years: If we're trying to reach a sight-and-sound generation (and we are), then where, oh, where are our sights and sounds in today's church? What do our sights and sounds need to look like in order to meet emerging trends? Let's face it: For most of us, our media needs an overhaul. I believe in outreach, but the church needs to be ready to hold on to the "unreached" when they walk through the church doors. At Church On The Move, we constantly evaluate what we're doing and what we need to fix within—that way, we can reach out to those who are searching, those who are questioning, and those who are returning after an absence. It stands to reason that what relates to today's kids will not be the choices of an older generation. This is where I want to remind you of Paul's words: "[Forget] the past and [look] forward to what lies ahead."

THE UNAVOIDABLE SUBJECT

Another emerging trend we must face involves safety. The world has sure changed since I was in Bible college. I never had a class that addressed safeguarding kids from sexual predators and violent crimes. Maybe some should have, but the need didn't seem as apparent back then. Today, on the other hand, that issue is front and center. The following statistics are unpleasant, but they can't be ignored—especially by those who've been called to children's ministry.

According to the U.S. Department of Justice Bureau of Statistics, approximately 4,300 child molesters were released from prisons in 15 states in 1994. An estimated 3.3 percent of these were rearrested for another sex crime against a child within three years of release from prison. Among those child molesters released in 1994, 60 percent were imprisoned for molesting a child 13 years old or younger. Another Department of Justice study revealed data on the rearrest, reconviction, and reimprisonment of 9,691 male sex offenders (including 4,295 child molesters), who were tracked for three years after their release from prisons in 15 states in 1994. Those 9,691 represented two-thirds of all male sex offenders released from prisons in the United States that year. Highlights of the study include the following:

- Within three years following their release, 5.3 percent of sex offenders were rearrested for another sex crime.

- Compared to non-sex offenders released from state prisons, released sex offenders were four times more likely to be rearrested for the same crime they'd been incarcerated for.

- The 9,691 released sex offenders included 4,295 men imprisoned for child molesting. (www.ojp.usdoj.gov/bjs/)

So many churches desperate for workers neglect to do their homework; they overlook the importance of "knowing them that labor among you." Since 1985, more than 400 convicted sex offenders had volunteered at the three churches where I'd been on staff. Today I spend more time safeguarding children by watching for and identifying known sex offenders than at any other time in my ministry. Unfortunately, this is one of our emerging trends—churches (regardless of location or size) will be forced to deal with the issue of safety as an ongoing program.

The problem isn't isolated to known offenders. Because I deal with more restraining orders and domestic violence issues at our church than ever before, we've increased our lines of communication between our pastoral ministries department, our security department, and our children's ministry. The societal trend of domestic imbalance has penetrated the church, and as a result we need to reprioritize how we view safety for our children.

A MOVEMENT TOWARD SATISFACTION

One more trend I've observed is the growing need to improve customer service for those who attend our churches. We only have the chance to make one first impression—for the church, that impression starts in the parking lot and continues until the service is over and the kids have been retrieved from their classrooms. The bottom line is, you gain those you serve! Improve first impressions of your ministry by considering these basic questions:

- How can we make the check-in process more family-friendly?

- How can we eliminate check-in lines so people aren't late to services?

- How can I improve communication on every level—from signage, to room-to-room connections, and even into the parking lot?

- How can I answer questions before they're even asked—so they don't need to be asked?

- How can I eliminate problems so that the children's ministry experience for families is a pleasant one?

Serving people is a choice—a conscious choice. Not only that, but it affects the majority of policy and procedure decisions. For us to reach young families, we must serve young families. That includes serving the most valuable possessions they have: their babies. It might mean we take a new look at lowering the ages of babies in each room to accommodate parents. It may mean we decorate our nurseries according to popular trends, in ways that appeal not only to toddlers but also to young mothers.

If we're going to reach this have-it-now, charge-it-don't-save-for-it, microwaveable, do-it-quick culture (whether or not we agree with their values), we must serve them. That includes taking their children's safety seriously, using extraordinary means to provide the best and healthiest care. It means we should explore ways to make church simple and satisfying. And to do all of those things in an impactive, memorable way, we need to forecast, anticipating the needs of our kids and the swings of their culture.

THE 21ST-CENTURY DIGITAL AGE

BY CRAIG JUTILA

The music gradually builds to a loud enough level that I wake up to greet the new day. I'd set the MP3 player to wake me at a set time and gradually increase the volume so as not to "startle" me awake as do some of the more unsophisticated alarms we're accustomed to. I saunter down the hallway and into the kitchen, where my cell phone is beeping. It's alerting me to the first e-mails of the day that have been routed to my phone from a server at church. I have breakfast, jump in the car with the kids, and we're on our way to school. As we go, we bop to the sounds of a popular Christian artist on my iPod. After dropping the kids off, I head to the local coffee establishment to catch up on some church-related things. I sit answering a few e-mails, and I watch an archived service from our church in the left-hand corner of my computer screen. Earphones in, e-mails on, and the service almost over, I take a sip of my latte, pull out my video iPod, and download the service to it, as well as a couple of other videos I purchased to watch at a later time.

Ladies and gentleman, welcome to the 21st-century digital age. Have you ever stopped to notice how much information is readily available to us today? We can download countless documents, music, and videos with a click. So how do we apply this new way of life to what we do at church? Or here's a much tougher question: Will the church want to adapt to this new way of life? There's much available in this digital age to help teachers and leaders of children enhance the message, not stifle it.

Separating our method from our message is sometimes confusing. Sure, we can all articulate the difference between the two, but when it comes right down to it, we're still teaching kids the same way we always have. Our methods haven't changed. Should we change? Yes. Why? Because kids today are different from kids of the last decade, and the decade before that, and the decade before that. Children today are more multifocused and are often overinvolved with various activities. Cell phones, cable television, and audio and video downloads are all a normal part of their lives, and they *expect* this level of fast information. The world has grown smaller, quicker, and more available. Never mind fast food—fast information is now the precedent. And technology is changing at light speed. Just ask a child what a CD is. Most of them today don't know—it's as outdated as (I hate to date *myself* here) the 8-track.

I recently noticed an advertisement offering a conference for executives who market information to children. The title of the conference was "Brand-Building in the Kids' Digital Space." Some of the content to be discussed was mobile TV, mobile content, mobile and Web-based messaging, podcasting, and video casting (just to name a few). These adults' focus in business is how to market to children. Case in point: When my family is out to eat at a restaurant, one of our children will often ask, "Dad, can I play on your phone?" What do we need to do to make a difference using this technology?

Let's take a look at education in the United Kingdom. The secretary of education in the UK was recently asked what part technology plays in the education of children. Her response was, "We see its power to boost standards and enable every child to achieve their full potential" (Macworld, March 2006). The UK has jumped in with both feet, providing Web sites that combine video games, audio, and animation to stimulate learning. They continue to launch sites that allow children access to educational software while the child is at home.

As we launch into this 21st century, our methods of educating children must change. No longer will the lesson be left in the classroom. It'll be brought home with kids or downloaded when they get home. They'll put it on their video-playing device and take it to school to share with others who don't go to church. The question in the past had been *where* kids learn about Jesus. Now we must add *when* and *how* as well. The digital charge has begun, and it's time we utilize these various methods to our advantage in educating children.

Picture this at a church service: No longer will lessons be taught out of a book—they'll be on video. And not just lessons but games will be presented through video, too. Scores will be tallied and projected in a matter of seconds, letting students know if their answers are correct. Next you might have a video of a fifth-grade girl giving her testimony to her peers on how important it is to be honest at school and in relationships. After the service, children with their video iPods will walk over to a computer and, at the click of a button, will walk off with that day's lesson and testimony.

I'm not just talking about using video or Webcasting instead of going to church. I'm talking about using this technology to enhance church. The lesson is no longer left at church. It's in their back pockets, digitally. They watch it, show it to their friends, and learn from it again and again. I have my own video iPod securely fastened to the front of my car, and my kids enjoy watching a certain comedian on it. They've watched the video no fewer than 20 times, and they can recite the video to a T. Why not make it a lesson on honesty or forgiveness? Something creative that kids can watch over and over until they are matching the teacher's tone, inflection, and cadence perfectly. And, oh yeah, with a little truth thrown in to boot.

"When will this happen?" you ask. It already is—every weekend at our church and at churches across the country. Lessons aren't meant just for classrooms; they're meant for life and on demand—when we need them. And now we have the technology to put this into practice. Don't misunderstand: Nothing will ever replace the relationship a teacher brings to the student. I'll continue to stand on my soapbox and preach relationship over curriculum until I die, but let's use the technology available to us to further enhance the child's learning.

There's no doubt that controversy will surround the new technology and how we use it. Some will embrace it, some will try it, and still others will avoid it at all costs. We must, however, warm up to the fact that children are much more media-savvy than we were as kids, or might ever be. For the naysayers of the digital age, try this math: "You want to know how many [iPods] were sold in 2005 alone? *32 million*. At this rate of expansion, there will be an iPod for every man, woman, and child in the US by the end of 2008, and one for everyone on Earth by 2012" (Macworld, March 2006).

The direction for 21st-century communication has shifted from one dimension to three. We should seriously look at the advantages of digital lessons—they can be reviewed, rewatched, and recommunicated. If the content is solid, this will no doubt increase learning and give children a greater chance at not only understanding the lesson but also applying it in their lives every day.

I'll let you decide. Will it be flannel Moses or digital Moses this week for your 10-year-olds? You know what my vote is. How about yours?

Try This

BY DEBBIE GOWENSMITH

SONGS OF DIVERSITY

With each new generation, the U.S. population becomes more and more multiethnic. What does this mean for your children's ministry?

Gene Roehlkepartain, senior advisor at Search Institute, said this to Children's Ministry Magazine: "All children's ministry leaders need to re-examine their ministries to determine how welcoming and engaging they are to children and families from many different cultures."

One way to create a welcoming atmosphere in your classroom is to incorporate different languages into your regular song time. Children may have their own favorites to share, and you can also find music from different cultures in resources such as the songbooks *Global Praise 1* and *Global Praise 2* by Steven Kimbrough, and *The Faith We Sing* (www.cokesbury.com).

Activity 2

AROUND THE GLOBE

Help children understand that God loves people all over the world with this activity. If possible, download Google Earth on a laptop computer via the Internet at http://earth.google.com (click on "Get Google Earth: Free Version"). If you don't have Internet access or a laptop, hang a large wall map on a wall of your meeting space or bring in a globe. If using Google Earth, project the images onto a wall or projector screen using a projector.

Show your town on the map or on Google Earth. Then ask children if they know where their families—their parents, grandparents, great-grandparents, and so on—lived before they lived in this country, state, or city. When a child names a different place, "visit" that place by typing its name into Google Earth or by finding it on the map. If possible as you visit different places, discuss similarities and differences between it and your city—language, seasons, food, and so on. If you can access the Internet, you can even search for information about those different places. (You can often link to such information directly from Google Earth.) If you're using a map or globe that you can leave in the room, place a sticker on each place you visit together.

Read aloud Galatians 3:28: "There is no longer Jew or Gentile, slave or free, male and female. For you are all one in Christ Jesus." As you visit different places, you might lead children in saying something like, "There is no American or French, but we are all one in Christ Jesus" or "Jesus loves people from France." After visiting several countries, have children discuss these questions:

- **How do you feel when you see that people are from all these different places?**
- **What does it mean to you that God loves people from all of these different places?**
- **How can you show God's love to someone who is different from you this week?**

Activity 3

A FAMILY THAT SERVES TOGETHER...

Schools are learning that parental involvement in their children's classrooms can reinforce learning at home, and churches are starting to catch on. Although ideally each parent or caregiver would act as a co-teacher for Sunday school at least once per quarter, you can also use the following idea to invite parents into the classroom for a special project. Because so many different activities vie for families' time and attention and because the idea is to get parents involved in the classroom, it's best if this activity take place during Sunday school or another regular meeting time.

Tip

Set the date and send out invitations at least one month in advance, and then follow up at least once about a week before the date of this event.

Invite parents and other caregivers to Sunday school to give them a taste of what kids are involved in and also to encourage them to work together as a family to serve others. As a service project that is easy to do within the classroom, children and their parents will create letters of support for members of the military.

Well in advance of this event, see the Web sites http://www .americasupportsyou.mil/ or http://www.amillionthanks.org/How_To_ Mail.asp to find out how to send letters to members of the military. If people from within your church or larger community serve in the military, it's best to send the letters to them.

Because you want to demonstrate a fairly typical class for the parents, plan to follow the normal classroom schedule. As parents arrive, greet them and then direct them to whatever activity you normally have kids do while they're waiting for class to get started. Begin as you typically do, with a song or a prayer, for example.

When it's time for the day's lesson to begin, explain that one of Jesus' disciples, James, wrote a letter to help Christians who were having a hard time. James reminded the Christians to do what God's Word says (James 1:22) and that it says to "love your neighbor as yourself" (James 2:8). Tell them that today families are going to work together to follow James' example of helping others.

Explain that service members have to regularly leave their families to go to faraway places to serve the country. Have children discuss the following questions with their parents or caregivers:

- **What do you like best about being with your family?**
- **What do you think it would be like to be away from your family for a long time?**

After discussing, have children and their parents work together to write or draw letters to service members to thank them and encourage them. Debrief the experience with these questions:

- **How did it feel to help someone by writing a letter?**
- **What does it mean to you that you can work together to show God's love to someone?**
- **How can you and your family show love to someone else this week?**

Activity 4

TEACH YOUR CHILDREN WELL

As parents and other caregivers work more and more hours outside of the home, television, video games, the Internet, and other technologies have more and more opportunities to shape children's values. With this activity, get parents and caregivers involved in Sunday school and remind them that they are the essential role models in their children's lives. You may choose to use this for a special Mother's Day or Father's Day lesson.

Invite parents or caregivers to your Sunday school class or other regular meeting time. Have parents join in the regular flow of activities with their children. When it's time for this activity, have children turn to their parents or caregivers. Parents should think of a simple skill that they would like to teach their children, and then do their best to teach what they can right then. For example, a parent might use a ball of paper to teach a child how to throw a ball. For parents who are stumped, suggest that they teach how to write a cursive letter, spell a word, or tie a bow. Give parents five minutes to teach their children.

After five minutes, read aloud Deuteronomy 6:6-7 to the group: "And you must commit yourselves wholeheartedly to these commands that I am giving you today. Repeat them again and again to your children. Talk about them when you are at home and when you are on the road, when you are going to bed and when you are getting up." Then ask parents to spend the next five minutes teaching their children about a good behavior—telling the truth, being kind to others, and so on.

After five minutes, have parents and children discuss these questions:

- **Children, what was it like to learn from your parents? What other things have you learned from them?**
- **Parents, what was it like to teach your children?**
- **How was this activity like or unlike your daily life at home?**
- **Parents, what specific behavior do you want to model for your child over the next month?**
- **Children, how will you learn from your parents this month?**

Conclude by explaining that while video games, television, and the Internet are teaching children some ways of thinking about life, parents and other primary caregivers are still the most important role models for children.

As an alternative or additional activity to use during a holiday season, have parents work with their children to act out for the class a family tradition associated with that holiday. For example, a parent and child might sing Christmas carols if their family sings carols every Christmas Eve. After everyone has shared, have them discuss Deuteronomy 6:6-7. Then have families discuss the following questions:

- **Parents, what was it like to introduce a family tradition to your own children?**
- **Children, what was it like to teach a tradition to this group?**
- **How was sharing this tradition like or unlike teaching others about good behaviors?**
- **Parents, what values do you want to pass on to your children this** [holiday season]**?**
- **Children, how can you be sure to learn from your families this** [holiday season]**?**

Activity 5

JSS LUVS U

The way we communicate with each other is changing rapidly. Each new technology links people more speedily and more readily, but it also tends to remove us more from each other's physical company. We rely more and more on e-mail and text messages to stay in touch. How does this affect a child's understanding of God's Word? Use this activity to convey that although the format has changed, God's Word is still relevant today.

If possible borrow several cell phones to use in class; it's best to have one cell phone for every four to five children.

If you can't borrow cell phones, either use a laptop, a compatible projector, and a projection screen to project the text messages, or simply write the messages in large letters on a sheet of newsprint taped to a wall.

Type the following message into each of the cell phones so that the message appears on the phone's screen: "God luvd d wrld so much dat he gave Hs 1 & onlE Son, so dat evry1 hu BlEvs n him wiL not perish bt hav eternal Lyf."

Have children get into groups of four or five, and give each group a cell phone. Ask children to read the text message. Then give each group a Bible, and help them find and read John 3:16. Then ask them to discuss what the text message means to them.

While children talk, enter the following new text message into the phones so that the screens show this: "Do 2 othRz wutevA U wud llk dem 2 do 2 U." Give the phones back to the groups, and ask them what the message says. Help them find and read Matthew 7:12 from the Bible, then discuss what the verse means to them. Then ask:

- **How are these two kinds of communication different and alike?**
- **Does it make a difference to you whether you read a message from the Bible or in a text message? Why or why not?**
- **If you want to tell someone why you love Jesus, how would you tell that person?**

Have each group type into the cell phone a text message that tells one reason they love Jesus. If kids are uncomfortable or unfamiliar with the technology, they can write or draw their messages on newsprint. When groups are finished, have them pass the cell phones or newsprint messages to another group, then another, and so on, until all groups have had a chance to read all the messages. Then have each group say its message in unison. After that, have groups discuss these questions:

- **What was it like to share a message about Jesus?**
- **How was that like reading about Jesus in the Bible or on a text message?**

Explain that although the way we communicate changes, the truth that Jesus loves us is true today just as it was when the Bible was written. Have children each decide one way they will tell others about Jesus this week.

Activity 6

PICTURES WORTH A THOUSAND WORDS

Children are becoming increasingly technologically savvy at younger and younger ages. Even if they don't have their own cell phones or laptops yet—and many do—they see the world through a technological lens. Church activities like worship seem out of step with their world if they don't incorporate at least some elements of technology. At the same time, worship is more meaningful for children when they actively contribute. This activity uses a technological medium to encourage children to actively participate in worshipping God.

Bring at least one digital camera (one camera for every four to six children is even better), a laptop computer with PowerPoint, the compatible cords and software to download photos onto the computer, and a compatible projector. It's a bonus if the laptop can burn CDs or DVDs on-site.

Read aloud Psalm 8 to the children. Then ask:

• **Why do you think this writer wanted to say these things to God?**
• **Have you ever felt something like this for God? If so, when?**

Explain that when we show God our love, we are worshipping God. Ask children to call out different ways we can show God our love—prayer, singing, and so on.

Have children get into three groups (groups should include three to six children). Ask groups to discuss these questions:

• **Why do you love God?**
• **What do you see around you that makes you think of God?**

Explain that each group will have a chance to use the digital camera for five minutes to take pictures that show why they love God or what they see that makes them think of God. Then the group will think of a song to sing along with the photos and then think of actions to perform along with the song. Each group will have a chance to do all three things.

Give children a few minutes to plan what photos they want to take. Have a volunteer work with each group. One group should spend five minutes taking photos. The other groups can choose a worship song to sing and can practice singing it.

After five minutes, have groups rotate functions. Groups that have already chosen a song can now either create actions to go along with the worship song of their choice, or they can take pictures. Then switch roles again after another five minutes. Finally, gather children together.

While you download the photos onto the computer, have a volunteer lead children in singing a worship song such as "Awesome God."

After photos are downloaded, use the projector to show a slide show of all the photos. Then have each group take a turn performing their worship songs and motions with their photos repeating in the background.

After all groups have finished, lead kids in applauding God to close your worship time.

If you're able, burn a CD of the photos for each child to use in worshipping God at home.

Activity 7

ON FRIENDLY GROUND

Seeker-sensitive churches are realizing how intimidating it can be for someone who isn't very familiar with church to come to Sunday school or worship. Even children are more comfortable in places that feel familiar. So instead of having children invite their friends to church, use this outreach event to help your children invite their friends to meet Jesus in a less intimidating setting.

This event can be as simple or as elaborate as you desire. Have children invite their friends to Sunday school at a park close to the church. You can create or purchase invitations, if you wish, and have children deliver them a couple of weeks in advance. You likely will need to reserve a spot at the park several weeks in advance, as well as consult with your students' parents about providing rides to the park for children and their friends.

The event itself includes an icebreaker, a snack, and a game. You'll want to give the children some unstructured play time at the park as well. Remember that the idea is to help children introduce Sunday school and Jesus to their friends in a less intimidating way, so try not to speak with church jargon that new children won't understand.

As children arrive, allow them to play in a specified area of the park. When it's time to begin, call them all back together. Welcome everyone to Sunday school in the park, and explain that everyone should have fun today getting to know each other and learning something about Jesus.

Have the group sit in a circle, with one child standing in the middle of the circle. Explain that when standing in the middle of the circle, children must tell the group something about themselves or their families. Whoever has that fact in common must stand up, race across the circle, and try to find a new seat. The person in the middle also must try to find a seat, leaving one new person left in the middle. Children can say things like "I have two brothers" or "My favorite food is pizza." You may want to stand in the middle of the circle with children to give them ideas about what kind of information to share.

After about five minutes, have children sit down. Explain that just as we get to know people little by little before we are friends, we get to know Jesus little by little until we decide whether we want to be friends with him.

Tell kids that Jesus was a teacher, but he could also do wonderful miracles—better than what the best magicians in the world can do. Explain that while magicians use tricks to make it look like they can do wonderful things though they really can't, Jesus could *really* do miracles. Tell children that you're going to tell a story about one of those miracles and that you need their help. When you say the word "fish," children should move their arms in a swimming motion; when you say "bread," children should pretend to take a big bite from a sandwich; and when you say "crowd," kids should jump up as though trying to see over the heads of lots of people. Tell the story of Luke 9:10-17 using your own words, and include "fish," "bread," and "crowd" as often as possible.

Afterward, set out ingredients for sandwiches—bread, cheese, meat, condiments, and so on—as well as napkins, plastic knives, paper plates, and cups of juice. Ask the members of your Sunday school class to serve their visiting friends. Explain that Jesus teaches us to help each other even above helping ourselves. Be sure to thank God for the food before children eat.

After children have eaten, have them play a modified game of Tag. Explain that Jesus needed a few special friends to help him spread the word about how much God loves us and that the Bible says he "fished" for people. Have one child play "Jesus," and give that child a Hula-Hoop. Instead of tagging people, that child should try to capture players in the Hula-Hoop. (Make sure children are gentle while using the Hula-Hoop!) Once someone is captured, he or she gets to help "Jesus" tag others (just with a hand rather than another Hula-Hoop).

Have children play the game for five to 10 minutes. Then call kids together, and thank everyone for coming. Close with a prayer, thanking God for our friend Jesus and for the new friends you met today.

Activity 8

FROM ME TO YOU

Children spend hours interacting with computers, video games, and TV, but it's critical that they engage with other children in meaningful ways. Only through direct personal connection will they learn how to be a friend, how to accept and give help, how to encourage others, and so on. And how can children really know Jesus if they don't know how to personally connect with him or other people? This simple, ongoing project encourages that crucial interpersonal connection.

Bring a camera to class, and take each child's photo. If you use a Polaroid camera, you can create the project during the same session. Otherwise, print out a photo of each child and bring all the photos to the next session. If a camera and printer aren't available, children could draw portraits of each other instead.

On the day you have all the photos, explain that each corner of the room represents a number of hours spent doing activities: one corner represents less than one hour, a second corner represents one to two hours, a third represents two to three hours, and a fourth represents more than three hours. Tell children that you will name an activity, and then they should go to the corner that shows how many hours each day they spend doing that activity. When everyone understands, name the following activities one by one, allowing time for kids to move to the appropriate corners:

- Watching TV

- Playing video games

- Working or playing on a computer

- Playing and talking with friends

- Playing and talking with your family

Tell children that while video games and TV are fun, it's important that we learn how to be good friends. Read aloud 1 Thessalonians 5:11, and explain that you are going to practice encouraging each other.

Ask each child to tape his or her photo to a wall. Then distribute stickers and markers that will write on photos. Have kids line up and visit each photo, writing or drawing something encouraging on each one. For example, children could thank each other for being nice, or they could write that the person does something particularly well. (You may want to tape the pictures to sheets of papers so that there's enough room to write.) Afterward, give children time to read what others wrote about them before discussing these questions:

- **What was it like to encourage each other? What was it like to read those encouraging words?**
- **How was this like or unlike the way you feel when you play video games or watch TV?**
- **What will you do this week to encourage someone face to face?**

Activity 9

TRUTH IN ADVERTISING

Marketing messages target children beginning at an early age and then grow from there. The shows they watch, the clothes they wear, and even the programs at school—all come with marketing messages that encourage children to put their faith in products. If this message is not countered, children may grow up believing that problems can be solved and happiness can be found with the right product. Use this activity to lay a foundation in evaluating the myriad messages society aims at children.

Have children form groups of four or five. Distribute one or two children's magazines to each group, and ask the group to study the ads and name three ways advertisers try to sell things to them, such as making something look fun to play with. After a few minutes, ask each group to report what three things they noticed.

Then have each group choose an item that no one in the group likes to eat—cold oatmeal, for example. Ask groups to each create and act out an advertisement to try to convince other kids that eating that food would be good.

After five to 10 minutes, have each group perform its ad. Then ask:
- **What was it like to try to sell something you don't like?**
- **How do you feel when someone tries to make you want something?**

Read aloud Matthew 7:15. Then ask:
- **How are the ads you created like a wolf dressed up like a sheep?**
- **How can you tell whether something is dressed up in order to make you want it or believe someone?**
- **When someone is trying to make you want something, what will you do to decide whether you really need it?**

Read aloud Psalm 9:10. Then ask:
- **How do you feel to know that you can always trust God?**
- **How is the promise in this verse different from an ad?**

Remind children that people who create and pay for ads are just trying to sell things. The ads might not tell the whole truth about an item but often "dress up" the item so that it looks and sounds much better than it really is. That's why we can't always believe that an item in an ad will do for us everything the ad says. We can always believe God, though, because God has never broken a promise. Only God is not too good to be true!

Activity 10

A FACT'S A FACT

The trend over the past couple of generations has been more and more toward relativism—that no truth is absolute but instead fully depends upon each person's perspective. This message confuses children's thinking when it comes time for them to make choices about behaviors and values. This activity will introduce the idea that truth exists even though people experience things differently.

Have children get in pairs and sit back-to-back. Give one child in each pair an item such as a toy or a school supply without the other child seeing what it is. Then give children 30 seconds to describe the item without saying what it is so partners can try to guess what it is. Then have partners switch roles so that guessers become describers, and rotate items among partners so that no pair has the same item. Give the new describers another 30 seconds to describe the new items. Afterward, gather children together and ask these questions:

- **What was it like to guess what the hidden item was?**
- **Did you and your partner always see things the same way? Explain.**
- **How was this like trying to know what is true and what is opinion?**

Have partners sit back-to-back again and take turns describing Jesus to each other in 30 seconds. Then ask:

- **Was describing Jesus harder or easier? Why?**
- **How can you tell what is true about Jesus and what is opinion?**

Explain that sometimes people see things differently and so have different opinions. But truth is different from opinion. Truth is a fact that doesn't change.

What's the Truth?

Use a DVD player and a TV to show the clip from the movie *Toy Story* (Disney/Pixar, 1995) in which Woody tries to convince Buzz Lightyear that Buzz is only a toy. Ask kids to name which is fact and which is opinion between these two statements:

- **Buzz Lightyear is a toy.**
- **Buzz Lightyear is not a toy.**

Then ask:

- **How do you think Woody felt in this clip? How do you think Buzz felt?**
- **How is that like or unlike the way you feel when you try to figure out what's true in life?**
- **How do you know the truth about who Buzz is?**

Read aloud Matthew 16:13-16. Ask:

• **How can you decide what is true about who Jesus is?**

• **How can you decide whether something in life is true or not?**

Explain that people see the same things differently because of how they feel or what they've been taught. Buzz didn't think he was a toy, but he was a toy. Some people say Jesus is not the Son of God, but he is the Son of God. Some things in life are true all the time and are true for everyone.

Copyright Laws

Movie clips under three minutes are technically covered under the fair use doctrine (which allows portions of a work to be exhibited for educational purposes). But to be on the safe side, you can obtain a license for a small fee from Christian Video Licensing International. Visit www.cvli.org for more information. (You can't charge admission to a function where you screen clips.)